THE TEACHING OF "HUMANAE VITAE":
A DEFENSE

THE TEACHING OF "HUMANAE VITAE": A DEFENSE

"Every Marital Act
Ought to Be Open to New Life":
Toward a Clearer Understanding
by
Germain Grisez, Joseph Boyle,
John Finnis, and William E. May

and

Contraception and the Infallibility of
the Ordinary Magisterium
by
John C. Ford, S.J., and Germain Grisez

IGNATIUS PRESS   SAN FRANCISCO

Cover by Roxanne Mei Lum

With ecclesiastical approval
(The granting of the Imprimatur does not imply
acceptance of the theological opinions of the authors.)
© 1988 Ignatius Press, San Francisco
All rights reserved
ISBN 0-89870-214-3
Library of Congress catalogue number 88-81275
Printed in the United States of America

CONTENTS

General Introduction, by Germain Grisez   7

"Every Marital Act Ought to Be Open to New Life": Toward a Clearer Understanding, by Germain Grisez, Joseph Boyle, John Finnis, and William E. May   33

Contraception and the Infallibility of the Ordinary Magisterium, by John C. Ford, S.J., and Germain Grisez   117

GENERAL INTRODUCTION
by Germain Grisez

This book defends the Catholic Church's teaching on contraception, which is the central subject of Pope Paul VI's encyclical, *Humanae vitae*. Our focus throughout is on the *teaching* rather than on the *document*. The controversy which preceded and followed Pope Paul's publication of the document gave it unique historical importance. However, the profound theological importance of *Humanae vitae* is in the Catholic teaching that it reaffirms—what the encyclical calls "the moral doctrine on matrimony, proposed by the Magisterium of the Church with constant firmness".[1]

Focusing on the document, many media reports confused matters by suggesting that *Humanae vitae* announced a mere authoritative decision on the part of Paul VI: "Vatican Edict Condemns Birth Control", "Pope Bans Pill", and so on. Of course, if nothing more than a papal decision were in question, a subsequent decision might approve the use of contraception, and meanwhile the obligation to obey a merely human directive would be limited. Therefore, such

---

[1] *Humanae vitae*, 6, *AAS* 60 (1968): 484. "Magisterium" refers to the Pope and other bishops in communion with him, acting not as governors or leaders of the Church, but as teachers and preachers of the truth of faith and the Christian way of life.

reports encouraged people both to hope for an eventual change of policy and to consider themselves free to disregard what some dissenting theologians disparagingly referred to as the "current official Church teaching".

But focusing on the teaching, the encyclical itself makes it clear that what is in question is no mere decision or policy. Pope Paul had felt bound to reexamine the received teaching because of the various objections to it and, above all, because of the suggestion that use of the "pill" might not be a form of that contraception which has always been condemned. But careful study only confirmed the truth of what the Church always had taught and made it clear that the "pill" is morally the same as other forms of contraception. Thus, in writing *Humanae vitae*, Paul VI did not think he was deciding a matter of policy but that he was teaching a truth. He made this point when he said that married couples "should conform their deeds to God the Creator's guidance, which is expressed by the very nature of matrimony and its acts and which is declared by the constant teaching of the Church".[2]

Correctly understood, Catholic teaching excludes neither every sort of birth regulation nor every use of the pill. Abstaining from sexual intercourse on the days when the woman is fertile is an effective way of regulating births, and the Church's teaching does not exclude that method. The pill sometimes is prescribed to treat certain pathological conditions, and the Church's

[2] Ibid., 10, 488.

teaching does not exclude that use, even when it has the side effect of impeding conception.[3] What the Church's teaching concerning contraception does exclude is *any act intended to impede procreation*.[4] The teaching also is expressed in an affirmative way in *Humanae vitae* and in other, more recent documents of the Magisterium: <u>Every marital act ought to be open to new life.</u>[5]

The defense of this Catholic teaching is the common objective of the two theological articles reprinted in this book. But they defend it in different ways, since theologians who dissented from the Church's teaching raised two distinct sets of issues.

First, the dissenting theologians argued that the Church's teaching is incoherent insofar as it excludes contraception but accepts birth regulation by periodic abstinence. Assuming that the Magisterium is right about periodic abstinence, they urged it to admit that the tradition has been wrong about contraception. Many who shared this view also treated contraception as if the issue of its morality could be isolated from other moral issues. This attempt to isolate the issue of

[3] Ibid., 15–16, 491–92.

[4] Ibid., 14, 490. This section makes it explicit that two things make no difference to the morality of the act intended to impede procreation: (1) whether the act in question is carried out before intercourse (e.g., taking the pill) or during it (e.g., using a diaphragm or condom) or afterward (e.g., washing out the vagina); and (2) whether the intent to impede procreation is directed simply toward that as an end in itself or (as is commonly the case) toward some ulterior end.

[5] See below, 35, n. 1.

the morality of contraception was a key element in the argument offered for accepting contraception by some members of Pope Paul VI's Commission for the Study of Problems of Population, Family, and Birthrate. They maintained that the approval of contraception would be a legitimate development of traditional Christian moral teaching, not a fundamental reversal in it, and so would leave the remainder of the Church's moral teaching intact.

In response to these claims, Joseph Boyle, John Finnis, William E. May, and I try to clarify the Church's teaching concerning contraception, using as our point of departure the affirmative formulation: Every marital act ought to be open to new life. We lay out what we think is the most basic, intrinsic reason why it is always wrong to choose to do something to impede procreation—namely, that this choice necessarily is contralife—and we show that in this respect birth regulation by periodic abstinence is not morally equivalent to contraception. In doing this, we also show how the Church's teaching on contraception is tightly interwoven with her entire moral teaching concerning sex, marriage, and innocent life. Thus, the question of the morality of contraception cannot be treated in isolation.

In addition to the questions dissenting theologians raised about the truth of the Church's teaching concerning contraception and that teaching's relationship to other moral teachings, they also questioned the status of those teachings by asking how certain those teachings are. Such teachings, they claimed, have not been proposed infallibly and are not matters of faith; therefore, they concluded, such teachings could be mistaken. Sometimes dissenting theologians put this point metaphorically by saying that this body of moral teaching does not belong to the core of the gospel to which the Church is irrevocably committed.

In response, John C. Ford, S.J., and I try to show that the traditional teaching concerning contraception cannot be mistaken and does pertain to faith, because even if the Church has never solemnly defined it, she has proposed it infallibly. Our argument does not begin by trying to prove that the teaching on contraception is divinely revealed. Instead, we begin from Vatican II's teaching that the bishops spread around the world do teach infallibly under certain conditions. We try to show from the Council's documents precisely what those conditions are and from historical evidence that they were in fact met by the teaching on contraception. The point of our argument is not to insist on the Magisterium's authority but to show that the traditional teaching on contraception does pertain to faith and that the Church is irrevocably committed to it.

Ford's and my article was first published in 1978.[6] Readers of this book may be interested in some of the theological reactions it provoked, how we responded to those reactions, and the relationship between our thesis and some more recent pronouncements of the Magisterium.

[6] "Contraception and the Infallibility of the Ordinary Magisterium", *Theological Studies* 39 (1978): 258–312.

Perhaps the most important theological reaction to Ford's and my article was the critique by Francis A. Sullivan, S.J., in his book on the Magisterium.[7] Denying that the Church can teach *any* specific moral norm infallibly but accepting other presuppositions of our argument, Sullivan tried to show that it fails in various ways. I replied at length to Sullivan's criticisms.[8] It seemed to me they showed the need for only one easily made amendment to the argument that Ford and I develop. I shall indicate that amendment now rather than change the text reprinted below.

One of the conditions which must be met if a teaching is to be recognized as infallibly proposed is that it be taught as something to be held *definitively*—that is, as absolutely certain. Ford and I state four reasons for thinking that this condition was met by the Church's teaching on contraception. One of these reasons is that the teaching on contraception has always been that acts chosen to impede procreation are the matter of grave sin, and that such a teaching surely was proposed as certain.[9] Sullivan points out: "It is one thing to teach that something involves a serious moral obligation; it is quite another to claim that this teaching is now absolutely definitive, and demands an irrevocable assent."[10]

---

[7] Sullivan, *Magisterium: Teaching Authority in the Catholic Church* (New York: Paulist, 1983), 140–52.

[8] Grisez, "Infallibility and Specific Moral Norms: A Review Discussion", *Thomist* 49 (1985): 248–87.

[9] See below, 163–64.

[10] Sullivan, *Magisterium*, 147.

I concede the logical correctness of Sullivan's point, but deny its relevance to the teaching on contraception. To show its irrelevance, I supply a missing premise to complete the consideration Ford and I advance: Most Catholic pastors and teachers try to avoid putting unnecessary burdens on the faithful, and so they almost always observe a norm—one stated by many Doctors of the Church—which forbids unqualifiedly asserting anything to be a grave matter unless it certainly is so. With this additional premise, I argue that no "sin was included all over the world in Christian lists of mortal sins unless the norm excluding that kind of act was received, held, and handed on as an inescapable requirement of God's plan for Christian life—not merely as 'morally certain' but as undoubted—to be held definitively".[11]

Garth L. Hallett, S.J., also directly challenged Ford's and my thesis insofar as we claim that the universality required for infallible teaching was realized in the case of the received teaching on contraception.[12] He deployed a theory concerning what is necessary for agreement in one moral judgment and tried to show that the history of Catholic teaching on contraception did not meet the requirement set by that theory. I replied by arguing that Hallett's theory has no solid theological grounds and that his historical arguments are seriously defective.[13] However, this exchange pointed to the

---

[11] Grisez, "Infallibility and Specific Moral Norms", 283.

[12] "Contraception and Prescriptive Infallibility", *Theological Studies* 43 (1982): 629–50.

[13] "Infallibility and Contraception: A Reply to Garth Hallett", *Theological Studies* 47 (1986): 134–45.

need for another amendment to the argument Ford and I develop. Once more, I shall indicate that amendment now and leave the text unchanged.

In summarizing Vatican II's statement of the condition of universality, Ford and I say:

> What sort of evidence of the required universality can we expect and should we demand? The evidence must be this: that a certain point of teaching has been proposed by bishops repeatedly, in different times, in different places, in response to different challenges, that the bishops have articulated and defended this point of teaching in different intellectual frameworks, perhaps reinforcing it with varying disciplinary measures. Moreover, there must be no evidence that the point of teaching has ever been questioned or denied by any bishop or by anyone else authorized to participate in the Church's teaching mission without eliciting an admonition and a reaffirmation of what had been universally taught.[14]

Here we overstated the evidence needed for the universality required for an infallible exercise of the ordinary Magisterium. For although it does take some stretch of time for the bishops in communion with the Pope to agree in one judgment and to teach accordingly, universality does not depend on constancy in teaching over a time longer than that stretch nor does it require constancy under all the diverse conditions which we mentioned. We obviously formulated our summary with an eye to the history of the Church's teaching on

---

[14] See below, 149.

contraception. Therefore, granted (not conceded) that history does not show the condition of universality fulfilled in a way which meets the requirement as we overstated it, evidence that the bishops during *any* period agreed in one judgment on the morality of contraception is sufficient. And there is such evidence, as Ford and I show.

In the same issue of *Theological Studies* in which Ford's and my article first appeared, Joseph A. Komonchak published an article that did not explicitly mention ours but did include criticism of the argument we propose.[15] (Our article was submitted for publication well in advance, and Komonchak had about a year to study it.) Ford and I found only one point in Komonchak's criticism that we thought we could not ignore. That point was in a single paragraph in which Komonchak asserted that unless one engaged in a study similar to Noonan's, it would be simply dogmatic to disagree with Noonan's view, namely, that the approval of contraception could be a legitimate development of the tradition.[16] Ford and I had reserved the right to reply briefly in the same issue to Komonchak's critique, and we did so by adding one footnote to our article.[17]

Sullivan subsequently developed his criticisms along the lines of some other points Komonchak had made without bringing them to bear on Ford's and my argument. Thus, much of my reply to Sullivan also can be

[15] "*Humanae Vitae* and Its Reception: Ecclesiological Reflections", *Theological Studies* 39 (1978): 238–50.

[16] Ibid., 248.

[17] See below, 182, n. 73.

read as an expansion of our very brief reply to Komonchak.

Ford's and my article was translated into German and published as a booklet.[18] Joachim Piegsa, professor of moral theology at Augsburg, published a critique,[19] which provoked further discussion, in which Piegsa's many misstatements of fact were corrected and his arguments ably answered.[20] Several of Piegsa's arguments are similar to those which Sullivan later offered, and so, once more, my reply to Sullivan can be used to supplement the replies that others made to Piegsa.[21]

In our article, Ford and I explicitly assume that the Catholic Church enjoys the gift of infallibility, that this gift extends to certain moral norms in respect to

---

[18] *Das unfehlbare ordentliche Lehramt der Kirche zur Empfängnisverhütung*, trans. Rhaban Haacke, O.S.B. (Siegburg: F. Schmitt, 1980).

[19] "Hat das ordentliche Lehramt zur Empfängnisregelung unfehlbar gesprochen?" *Theologie der Gegenwart* 24 (1981): 33–41.

[20] See Gustav Ermecke, "Untrüglich wahr und verbindlich", and Rhaban Haacke, O.S.B., "Ein Widerlegungsversuch misslingt: Um das Lehramt und seine Aussage zur Empfängnisverhütung", in *Nicht Unfehlbar?* ed. Johannes Bökmann (Abensberg: Josef Kral, 1981), 33–42; 43–57.

[21] Another critic, F. J. Elizari, "The Ten Years of 'Humanae Vitae'", *Theology Digest* 28 (1980): 33–34 (which was digested from "A los diez años de '*Humanae vitae*': Boletin bibliogràfico", *Moralia: Revista de ciencias morales* 1 [1979]: 239–42), raised five points. Ford and I anticipated the first three, the fourth ignores our use of Noonan (which considerably reduces the need to provide data about the tradition), and the fifth is a question-begging argument based on the authority of theologians and the confusion of some episcopal conferences after *Humanae vitae*.

specific kinds of acts, and that the gift is operative in the teaching of the ordinary Magisterium under the conditions articulated by Vatican II.[22] Many dissenting theologians undoubtedly disagree with one or more of these assumptions; they did not think it necessary to take our argument seriously. I have treated many of these wider and more fundamental issues in works published since 1978.[23]

But there are signs that many dissenting theologians will not take seriously *any* argument against their position. Richard A. McCormick, S.J., commented on the pair of articles published by Komonchak and by Ford and me: "It is noteworthy that these two studies are basically essays in ecclesiology. [Note omitted.] It would be immodest for a moral theologian to attempt to referee such a dispute, though it is clear that many theologians (what Komonchak calls 'something like a *consensus theologorum*') would favor the Komonchak thesis."[24] Since Komonchak's article appeared in the

---

[22] See below, 127.

[23] See *The Way of the Lord Jesus*, vol. 1: *Christian Moral Principles*, with the help of Joseph M. Boyle, Jr., Basil Cole, O.P., John M. Finnis, John A. Geinzer, Jeannette Grisez, Robert G. Kennedy, Patrick Lee, William E. May, and Russell Shaw (Chicago: Franciscan Herald, 1983), chaps. 6, 23, 35, and 36; "Moral Absolutes: A Critique of the View of Josef Fuchs, S.J.", *Anthropos* 1 (1985): 155–201.

[24] "Current Theology: Notes on Moral Theology: 1978", *Theological Studies* 40 (1979): 89. McCormick goes on (89–90) to argue from Karl Rahner's authority that the norm concerning contraception pertains to concrete human nature, which is subject to change, and so that norm could not be proposed infallibly. For a critique of this position of Rahner's, see my *Christian Moral Principles*, 859, 869.

same issue of *Theological Studies* as ours, and since McCormick was commenting on both, neither Komonchak nor McCormick could have been referring to a consensus of opinion about our work among those who had *studied* it. Rather, their invocation of a consensus meant that they were sure that the position Ford and I defended would continue to be rejected by theologians who had not yet read our argument. In other words, Komonchak and McCormick manifested an attitude prevalent among dissenting theologians: Never mind arguments; we are in control here.[25]

Despite the stubborn conviction of dissenting theologians based on their own consensus, the Magisterium has not abandoned its defense of the traditional Catholic teaching on contraception.

Not only has John Paul II repeatedly reaffirmed the teaching personally, but under his leadership the Synod of Bishops of 1980 aired the issues fully and reached substantial agreement. This was expressed in a series of propositions which the Synod Fathers delivered to the Pope with the request that he prepare a synthetic document. In response he published the apostolic exhortation, *Familiaris consortio*, in which he cited the relevant synodal proposition and reaffirmed "in

---

[25] This unwillingness of dissenting theologians to listen to the argument and to try to respond to it was shared by Charles Curran. At the beginning of a book he published in 1982, *Moral Theology: A Continuing Journey* (Notre Dame, Ind.: University of Notre Dame Press, 1982), he discussed the relationship between the Magisterium and theology; in delimiting the subject to be treated, he blandly claimed that "all admit that the investigations of theologians have not involved the infallible teaching office of the Church" (5).

continuity with the living tradition of the ecclesial community throughout history . . . the Church's teaching and norm, always old yet always new, regarding marriage and regarding the transmission of human life".[26]

This reaffirmation, joining the authority of the Pope with that of a representative segment of all the bishops—"gathered together with the Successor of Peter *in the unity of faith*" (emphasis added)—surely is more authoritative than the statements of a minority of the national conferences of bishops. Thus, by the collaboration of the 1980 session of the Synod and John Paul II, the Magisterium regained some degree of solidarity and rendered obsolete whatever dissenting theologians found useful in the episcopal statements that had been hastily prepared and issued in the wake of *Humanae vitae*.

John Paul II's phrase, "in continuity with the living tradition of the ecclesial community throughout history", suggests his position on the status of the Catholic teaching concerning contraception. Elsewhere, the

---

[26] John Paul II, *Familiaris consortio*, 29, *AAS* 74 (1982): 115. The Pope cites synodal proposition 21: "This Sacred Synod, gathered together with the Successor of Peter in the unity of faith, firmly holds what has been set forth in the Second Vatican Council (cf. *Gaudium et spes*, 50) and afterwards in the Encyclical *Humanae Vitae*, particularly that love between husband and wife must be fully human, exclusive and open to new life (*Humanae Vitae*, 11; cf. 9, 12)." To this the Pope appends the note: "Section 11 of *Humanae Vitae* ends with the statement: 'The Church, calling people back to the observance of the norms of the natural law, as interpreted by her constant doctrine, teaches that each and every marriage act must remain open to the transmission of life.'"

20 THE TEACHING OF HUMANAE VITAE

Pope makes his position fully explicit. Nearing the end of a four-year-long catechesis on the redemption of the body and on marriage, he comments on *Humanae vitae*, noting that Paul VI stressed that the norm concerning contraception pertains to natural law, whose interpretation is within the Magisterium's competence. Pope John Paul then adds:

> However, we can say more. Even if the moral law, formulated in this way in the Encyclical *Humanae Vitae*, is not found literally in Sacred Scripture, nonetheless, from the fact that it is contained in Tradition and—as Pope Paul VI writes—has been "very often expounded by the Magisterium" (*HV*, no. 12) to the faithful, it follows that this norm *is in accordance with the sum total of revealed doctrine contained in biblical sources* (cf. *HV*, no. 4).
>
> It is a question here not only of the sum total of the moral doctrine contained in Sacred Scripture, of its essential premises and general character of its content, but of that fuller context to which we have previously dedicated numerous analyses when speaking about the "theology of the body".
>
> Precisely against the background of this full context it becomes evident that the above-mentioned moral norm belongs not only to the natural moral law, but also to the *moral order revealed by God*: also from this point of view, it could not be different, but solely what is handed down by Tradition and the Magisterium and, in our days, the Encyclical *Humanae Vitae* as a modern document of this Magisterium. [Emphasis his.][27]

---

[27] John Paul II, General Audience, July 18, 1984; *Insegnamenti di Giovanni Paolo II*, vol. 7, part 2 (Rome: Libreria Editrice Vaticana, 1984), 102; *L'Osservatore Romano*, Eng. ed., July 23, 1984, p. 1.

Here John Paul II reasons from the manner in which the Church has taught concerning contraception to that teaching's being consonant with the whole of revealed doctrine, and then from relevant contents of Scripture, which he had expounded in detail, to the norm's belonging to the "moral order revealed by God". This papal view wholly agrees with and strongly confirms the thesis for which Ford and I argued: that the traditional teaching concerning contraception somehow pertains to faith because the Church has proposed it infallibly.

If the Church's teaching concerning contraception really is a matter of faith, there is no room for dissent from it. Yet theological dissent continues, and dissenting opinions are accepted by many Catholics, including some bishops and priests, especially in the United States and other affluent nations. Thus, the Church is divided, with serious consequences.

The situation would be bad enough if the division were limited to the Church's teaching on contraception. But, as I said above, Boyle, Finnis, May, and I show that the issue of the morality of contraception cannot be isolated from the whole set of moral issues concerning sex, marriage, and innocent life.

Proponents of contraception in the 1960s could plausibly deny this; today, virtually every theologian who dissents from the Church's teaching on contraception also rejects other relevant moral absolutes and so asserts that it is *sometimes* morally acceptable to seek sexual satisfaction outside marriage (masturbation, fornication, homosexual relations, and so on), to attempt remarriage as if a sacramental marriage had been dissolved by divorce, and deliberately to kill the innocent (especially the unborn).[28]

Moreover, a 1987 public opinion poll reports not only that 66% of Catholics in the United States believe one can be a good Catholic without obeying the Church's teaching on contraception but also that 57% answer similarly with respect to remarriage after divorce and 39% with respect to abortion.[29] Other polls indicated that by 1985, 66% of Catholics in the United States wanted the Church to allow divorced Catholics to remarry and 58% approved of premarital intercourse.[30]

---

[28] See my *Christian Moral Principles*, 873. The letter of Joseph Cardinal Ratzinger, Prefect of the Congregation for the Doctrine of the Faith, to Rev. Charles Curran (July 25, 1986), *L'Osservatore Romano*, Eng. ed., August 25, 1986, p. 3, summarily lists the areas of Curran's dissent: "The indissolubility of consummated sacramental marriage, abortion, euthanasia, masturbation, artificial contraception, premarital intercourse and homosexual acts." As Curran's defenders pointed out repeatedly, while he has stated dissenting opinions more bluntly than some other theologians, his views are "in the mainstream" of Catholic theology in the United States. Part of Curran's self-defense was: "In our correspondence I have pointed out that many other theologians hold similar positions and that it is an injustice to me and harmful to the credibility of the Church and its hierarchical teaching office to single me out when so many others throughout the world hold similar positions" (*Faithful Dissent* [Kansas City, Mo.: Sheed and Ward, 1986], 266).

[29] See the Gallup poll conducted for and published in *National Catholic Reporter*, September 11, 1987, p. 8.

[30] See George Gallup, Jr., and Jim Castelli, *The American Catholic People: Their Beliefs, Practices, and Values* (Garden City, N.Y.: Doubleday, 1987), 51, 182.

Until very recently all Catholics believed and all Catholic teachers taught that most, if not all, of this body of moral teaching concerning sex, marriage, and innocent life is explicitly revealed. Various passages of Scripture support that belief, and a broader study, such as that conducted by John Paul II, uncovers many intrinsic links between these moral teachings and truths of faith concerning the human person, interpersonal relationships, the Fall, and redemption. The Church's teaching concerning the indissolubility of sacramental, consummated marriage was in fact defined by the Council of Trent.[31] Thus, treating this body of traditional moral teaching as if it were an outdated set of rules which can now be replaced by a more convenient, up-to-date set of rules leads to setting aside not only Vatican II's ecclesiology but that Council's and Vatican I's teaching concerning divine revelation itself.[32]

There is yet another sign, plain enough for anyone with eyes to see, that the traditional morality is no

---

[31] See my *Christian Moral Principles*, 848. Curran and other dissenting theologians claim that they dissent only from noninfallible teachings; in his letter to Curran (*L'Osservatore Romano*, Eng. ed., August 25, 1986, p. 3), Cardinal Ratzinger answers that claim not only by pointing out that the teaching on divorce and remarriage has been defined by Trent and that not all dissent from noninfallible teaching is acceptable, but also by pointing to Vatican II's teaching on the infallibility of the ordinary Magisterium: "First of all, one must remember the teaching of the Second Vatican Council which clearly does not confine the infallible Magisterium purely to matters of faith nor to solemn definitions." Ford and I use this Vatican II teaching as the major premise of our argument.

[32] See my *Christian Moral Principles*, 848, 894–97.

mere set of rules but part of God's revealed moral order—his wise and loving plan for salvation and happiness. It was not believing Jews and Christians but nonbelieving humanists who first proposed the new morality as part of their agenda for liberating human persons and building a wonderful new world.[33] From sexual reform they anticipated very great benefits. But as their proposed sexual revolution has been carried out, its costs have mounted, despite vast efforts at "sex education" and greatly enhanced techniques for controlling the various unwanted side effects of sexual behavior. Moreover, the anticipated benefits have not been realized. Instead, the new morality encourages sexual experimentation by children, evacuates intimate relationships of their deep meaning, destabilizes marriages, deprives children of the nurture of both parents acting in solidarity, imposes on society the costs of supporting children whose fathers do not support them, robs the most defenseless children of their very lives, and spawns a plague of sexually transmitted diseases.

In this situation, what are those Catholics to do who accept the truth of the traditional teaching concerning sex, marriage, and innocent life? What are the pastors of the Church to do who believe that this teaching pertains to faith?

Faithful Catholics in general, of course, should continue to act consistently according to the truth that

[33] See, for instance, World League for Sexual Reform, *Sexual Reform Congress: London, 1929* (London: Kegan, Paul, Trench, Trubner, 1930); *Sexual Reform Congress: Vienna, 1930* (Vienna: Elbemühl, 1931).

they accept, to bear witness to it, and to hand it on to their children. And there are encouraging signs that they are doing so. For example, a poll of Catholics in the United States, taken shortly after the publication of *Humanae vitae* in 1968, found 25% answering No to the question: Do you think it is possible to practice artificial methods of birth control and still be a good Catholic? The 1987 poll mentioned above, which was published exactly nineteen years later, found 27% answering No to an almost identical question.[34] The difference of two percentage points is hardly significant, but the constancy of this substantial minority's sense of faith is quite significant. Moreover, it is more impressive when one takes into account the fact that a large part of the population polled in 1968, including many of its more mature members, had died by 1987 and their places been taken by people too young in 1968 to be represented in a poll. Thus, it appears that the faithful not only are keeping the faith but handing it on despite unremitting contrary pressure from the surrounding culture and, in many cases, lack of effective leadership and support within the Church.

Pastors of the Church—the Pope, the other bishops, and all who assist in their pastoral service—who believe that the traditional teaching concerning sex, marriage, and innocent life pertains to faith should fully and consistently put what they believe into pastoral practice. There is a perennial temptation for the Church's pastors not to do that; St. Peter yielded to that temptation,

[34] See *National Catholic Reporter*, September 11, 1968, p. 9; September 11, 1987, p. 8.

and St. Paul rebuked him for it.[35] In the last section of our article, Boyle, Finnis, May, and I analyze and criticize four pastoral approaches to the use of contraception that we believe to be disastrously mistaken. Those who take the first three of those approaches are, I think, acting as Peter did.

Besides the aspect of pastoral practice which we discuss, there is another aspect in which, it seems to me, many of the Church's pastors are failing to put into practice what they believe. What I refer to is at the very heart of the crisis caused by dissent.

Within every ecclesiastical jurisdiction, from the Church universal to the humblest parish, many clerics and lay people, with and without theological training, say what they think and claim for it the status of legitimate Catholic opinion, even if it contradicts doctrine proposed by the Magisterium. The pastors of the Church need not (as a practical matter they physically or morally cannot) do anything about most such dissenting opinions.

But when a pastor *authorizes* others to teach and preach, he is personally responsible for what those whom he has authorized do with his authorization. Acting in and through those who teach and preach with his authorization, the pastor teaches and preaches dissent when those who act with his authorization do

---

[35] See Gal 2:11–16. The issue was *not*, as many trying to justify dissent from papal teaching have wrongly suggested in recent years, one of doctrine. Paul and Peter agreed on the doctrine, but Peter "acted insincerely", trying to placate opponents of the truth by not always acting in accord with it.

so, provided that he knows what they are doing and continues to authorize them to teach and preach when he could withdraw his authorization.

My point is not that dissenters who exercise various offices in the Church are abusing those offices and should be disciplined for doing so. That may be true, but it also may be true that dissenters are in good faith or that their abuse of office can be tolerated to avoid even greater evils. My present point is not even that those who dissent from the Church's teaching on sex, marriage, and innocent life are denying truths which pertain to faith and are leading people into sins and other great evils. I believe that is so, but the point I am now making would hold even if the Church's teaching were false and the opinions which dissent from it were based on a fresh divine revelation—as some who hold those opinions suggest by their talk of the Holy Spirit's work in the "sense of the faithful".

My point, rather, is that a pastor who believes the Church's teaching true and who himself teaches and preaches it is at the same time *himself* dissenting from that teaching when he does not withdraw his authorization to teach and preach from those who he knows are using it to teach and preach dissenting opinions. Such a pastor is contradicting himself, and there can be no justification for that inconsistency. Moreover, such inconsistency is a very grave matter, for by it a pastor both calls the faithful to conform their lives to difficult norms which concern grave matters and encourages the same faithful to set aside those norms and follow dissenting opinions. (Of course, only God knows the state of a pastor's heart; like any other sinner, he may be guilty of little or nothing due to lack of sufficient reflection.)

Consequently, every one of the Church's pastors should make it clear to all those who have his authorization to preach and teach that he cannot and will not tolerate their using that authorization to dissent from Catholic teachings which he himself accepts. Instead, as soon as it becomes evident that anyone having his authorization preaches or teaches dissenting opinions, he will withdraw the authorization, not to punish the one dissenting but to maintain his own integrity as a pastor.

In a letter to Charles Curran, Cardinal Ratzinger, as Prefect of the Congregation for the Doctrine of the Faith, wrote: "It must be recognized that the authorities of the Church cannot allow the present situation to continue in which the inherent contradiction is prolonged that one who is to teach in the name of the Church in fact denies her teaching."[36] That is an application in one particular case of the point I am making.

---

[36] Letter of September 17, 1985, *Origins* 15 (1986): 668. In his exchanges with the Congregation, Curran, *Faithful Dissent* (see n. 28), 152–53, 212–13, 266, invoked the "Norms of Licit Theological Dissent" stated by the National Conference of Catholic Bishops (United States), in *Human Life in Our Day* (Washington, D.C.: United States Catholic Conference, 1968), 18–19. At the same time, Curran plainly conceived his function as a theologian to be the exercise of a pastoral office, since he justified making dissent public by the theologian's obligation to make the dissenting position known to people so that they can put it into practice in their lives (64, 220). Hence, it is significant that Curran omitted an important one-

But the same principle applies to every one of the Church's pastors in respect to every individual he in any way authorizes to share in his pastoral ministry of teaching and preaching. Inconsistency between Rome and Washington which is intolerable, inasmuch as it destroys the Holy See's own integrity, cannot be tolerable within Rome, or Washington, or Germany, or any other jurisdiction in the Church.

While Ford and I do not explicitly say so, if our argument is sound, it shows that the traditional teaching concerning contraception could be solemnly defined. John Paul II's analyses lead to the conclusion that the norm belongs to "the moral order revealed by God", and this conclusion likewise shows that this norm could be solemnly defined. I have explained in another essay why it seems to me that some of the Church's teachings currently challenged by theological dissent should be defined. In that essay I also sketched out a possible procedure by which both theologians who defend opposite positions, and the bishops of the whole world, could play their proper parts in forging such definitions.[37] Here, I wish only to add that I do

---

sentence paragraph in the American bishops' 1968 norms: "Even responsible dissent does not excuse one from faithful presentation of the authentic doctrine of the Church when one is performing a pastoral ministry in Her name" (19).

[37] "How to Deal with Theological Dissent", *Homiletic and Pastoral Review* 87; part 1 (November 1986): 19–29; part 2 (December 1986): 49–61. See also Grisez, "The Definability of the Proposition: The Intentional Killing of an Innocent Human Being Is Always Grave Matter", in *Persona, Verità, e Morale: Atti del Congresso Internazionale di Teologia Morale*, Rome, aprile 7–12, 1986 (Rome: Città Nuova, 1987), 291–314.

not see how the Church's pastors can maintain (or recover) their integrity unless the Magisterium solemnly defines at least a few of the Church's contested moral teachings. The problem is twofold.

First, the status of these teachings has become clouded by dissent, so that many who share in pastoral responsibility undoubtedly are in good faith in thinking that they must at least make room for practice in accord with dissenting opinions. Hence, if a pastor were consistent, as I have argued he should be, in withdrawing his authorization from everyone who accepts dissenting opinions while acting with that authorization, that pastor would challenge many who are in good faith and provoke very strong reactions from all those in solidarity with them. (The reaction to the Congregation for the Doctrine of the Faith's handling of the Curran case is an example.) The painfulness of the consequences to everyone concerned makes overwhelmingly repugnant the option of doing what is necessary for pastoral integrity.

Second, some bishops openly share dissenting opinions and others plainly are sympathetic toward them. Thus, at present, the Church's teachers themselves are divided; the pastors of the Church and those who share in their ministry are not united in the same mind and the same judgment. In this state of affairs, communion is corruption; no pastor can maintain his own integrity without dividing himself from others. The traditional way for the Magisterium to deal with situations of this sort has been to face the issue squarely, to deal with it collegially, and to anathematize those who refuse to accept the consensus which takes shape concerning what "we all believed and taught".

If, as seems likely, the Holy See's policy for dealing with dissent since *Humanae vitae* has made the avoidance of schism a primary objective, the policy has failed. For while a large, openly declared schism has been avoided, many individuals are morally in schism; the ultimate authority they accept is what they call their own "conscience", but which in reality is nothing but a subjective judgment of what is and is not personally acceptable. Thus, only the institutional appearance of the unity of the Church is being saved, and the real situation of the Catholic Church today, especially in the affluent parts of the world, is remarkably like the situation St. Paul deplored in the Church of Corinth, where some said "I belong to Paul", others "I belong to Apollos", others "I belong to Cephas", and others "I belong to Christ".[38] Today some hope John Paul II will live a long time, while others look forward to the next pontificate; some hope that new appointments of bishops will tip the balance of certain national conferences while others do what they can to prevent that from happening.

Nobody should fear that if the Pope and the other bishops together undertook to resolve the moral issues which divide the Church they would fail to achieve their purpose. Jesus himself prayed for Peter and so assured him of the power to confirm the faith of his brother bishops. But until now, the situation has not

---

[38] Cf. 1 Cor 1:10–13.

been squarely faced; the Church has been acting like a person who suspects cancer and is putting off dealing with the problem. However, if the Pope and the other bishops set to work, one can be sure they will succeed. For then they will have undertaken their responsibility and they will pray for the light and power to fulfill it. They will receive what they ask, for Jesus promised to stay with his Church, and he is faithful. That is why Jesus sent the Holy Spirit, with a gift of certain truth.

Therefore, if the Pope and other bishops undertake their responsibility as teachers in the Church and judges of the Faith, surely they will come to agreement in the truth and will be able to announce to the world: It is the Holy Spirit's judgment and ours too . . . .

"Every Marital Act Ought to Be Open to New Life": Toward a Clearer Understanding

by

GERMAIN GRISEZ, JOSEPH BOYLE, JOHN FINNIS, and WILLIAM E. MAY

I. INTRODUCTION

One frequently encounters misinterpretations of the statement "Every marital act ought to be open to new life" and similar statements in recent Catholic teaching concerning contraception.[1] There are two common misinterpretations. One is: No couple may engage in marital intercourse without the intention to procreate. The other is: No couple may engage in marital intercourse at times when they think procreation is impossible. As interpretations of the Church's teaching, these must be mistaken. For the Church teaches that contraception is always wrong and that natural family planning (NFP) is not always wrong. But NFP facilitates intercourse without the intention to procreate at times when procreation is thought to be impossible. Moreover, the Church has never taught that marital intercourse is good only if the couple desire to procreate;

Reprinted with permission from *Thomist*, vol. 52, no. 3, July 1988.

[1] The proposition is formulated somewhat differently by Paul VI, *Humanae vitae*, 11, *AAS* 60 (1968): 488 (with references to *Casti connubii* and to Pius XII's Allocution to the Society of Italian Catholic Midwives); and by John Paul II, *Familiaris consortio*, 29, *AAS* 74 (1982): 115, following proposition 22 of the 1980 session of the Synod of Bishops. Moreover, the different formulations also are translated diversely. We do not think these differences matter for our present purpose.

indeed, couples known to be sterile have never been forbidden to marry.

We think that the only plausible interpretation of "Every marital act ought to be open to new life" is the following: It is wrong for those who engage in marital intercourse to attempt to impede the transmission of life, which they think their act otherwise might bring about. For if they do try to impede that to which their act of itself might lead, they choose to close it to new life.

Understood in this way, "Every marital act ought to be open to new life" expresses the same proposition as "Contraception is always wrong". Nevertheless, the affirmative formulation helps to clarify what contraception is, for it indicates the precise object of the contraceptive act. "Contraception" signifies only the prevention of *conception*, but the contraceptive act seeks to impede *the beginning of the life of a possible person*. The distinction is only conceptual, but we think it important, for the explicit reference to new life calls attention to the fact that contraception is a contralife act.

The characterization of contraception as a contralife act is one major element of the unbroken Christian Tradition condemning contraception as always wrong. For example, a canon, *Si aliquis*, concerning contraception was included in the Church's universal law from the thirteenth century until 1917: "If anyone for the sake of fulfilling sexual desire or with premeditated hatred does something to a man or to a woman, or gives something to drink, so that he cannot generate, or she cannot conceive, or offspring be born, let it be held as homicide."[2] This canon does not say that contraception is homicide; the Tradition made no such mistake. The canon rather says that contraception should be regarded as homicide is regarded. To regard contraception as homicide is regarded is not only to make it clear that contraception is wrong but also to point to its being contralife as the reason why it is wrong.

When contraception is regarded as contralife, it is seen as evil outside marriage as well as within. Historically, contraception probably was more common among the unmarried than the married, and much of the Tradition condemned contraception without distinguishing between its uses in and outside marriage. But *Casti connubii* dealt with contraception only within marriage, for marriage was that encyclical's subject. The argument in the Church in the 1960s dealt with contraception only within marriage, because those who were arguing for contraception said that they wanted only to justify its use in marriage, not to replace the whole traditional sex morality.

Recent Church teaching, focusing on the use of contraception within marriage, condemns it with specific

---

[2] *Decret. Greg. IX*, lib. V, tit. 12, cap. v; *Corpus iuris canonici*, ed. A. L. Richter and A. Friedberg (Leipzig: Tauchnitz, 1881), 2, 794: "Si aliquis causa explendae libidinis vel odii meditatione homini aut mulieri aliquid fecerit, vel ad potandum dederit, ut non possit generare, aut concipere, vel nasci soboles, ut homicida teneatur." Some translate "causa explendae libidinis", which is broad enough to cover all motivation by sexual impulse, "to satisfy lust", which unnecessarily limits the motive to habitual vice.

reference to marital acts and distinguishes it from NFP rightly practiced by married couples.

Opponents of this teaching almost always claim that contraception is morally indistinguishable from NFP, since, they say, both propose to prevent pregnancy. Confronted with this argument, one defending the Tradition either must show that contraception differs morally from NFP precisely in its relationship to the value of life, or must avoid grounding the immorality of contraception in its contralife character.

Recent Church teaching apparently takes the latter alternative. For although the Tradition pointed out contraception's contralife character, recent Church teaching focuses almost entirely on contraception's wrongness in relation to other values, especially chastity, marital love, and the sacred character of virtuous sexual activity in marriage.[3]

[3] Still, recent Church teaching does not entirely ignore contraception's contralife character. Paul VI, Homily on the Feast of Saints Peter and Paul, June 29, 1978, *AAS* 70 (1978): 397; *L'Osservatore Romano*, Eng. ed., July 6, 1978, 3, refers to *Humanae vitae* as a defense of life "at the very source of human existence"; recalls *Gaudium et spes*, 51, on abortion and infanticide; and adds: "We did no more than accept this charge when, ten years ago, we published the Encyclical *Humanae Vitae* (July 25, 1968; cf. *AAS* 60 [1968]: 481–503). This document drew its inspiration from the inviolable teachings of the Bible and the Gospel, which confirms the norms of the natural law and the unsuppressible dictates of conscience on respect for life, the transmission of which is entrusted to responsible fatherhood and motherhood." Also John Paul II, Homily at Mass for Youth, Nairobi, Kenya, Aug. 17, 1985; *Insegnamenti di Giovanni Paolo II*, vol. 8, pt. 2 (Rome: Libreria Editrice Vaticana, 1985), 453; *L'Osservatore Romano*, Eng. ed., Aug. 26, 1985, 5, points out that the fullest

We think, however, that while contraception is wrong for several reasons, it is wrong primarily and essentially because it is contralife. In this paper, we shall try to show that contraception and NFP fundamentally differ precisely in that contraception necessarily is contralife and NFP need not be. We shall also explain how other arguments against contraception are related to the one we consider fundamental. We hope that these clarifications will help to overcome some of the confusions occasioned by certain formulations in *Humanae vitae* and *Familiaris consortio*—formulations not of their central teachings but of their explanations both of why contraception is morally wrong and of why NFP can be morally acceptable.[4]

---

sign of self-giving is when couples willingly accept children; quotes *Gaudium et spes*, 50; and adds: "That is why antilife actions such as contraception and abortion are wrong and are unworthy of good husbands and wives."

[4] While the treatment in the present article supersedes our previous treatments of the precise points considered here, certain elements useful to fill out the present account of the morality of contraception and related questions can be found in some of our previous publications: Germain Grisez, *Contraception and the Natural Law* (Milwaukee: Bruce, 1964); "Marriage: Reflections Based on St. Thomas and Vatican Council II", *Catholic Mind* 64 (June 1966): 4–19; "Contraception and Reality", *Triumph*, in three parts: Feb. 1968, 21–24; Mar. 1968, 18–21; Apr. 1968, 27–30; *The Way of the Lord Jesus*, vol. 1, *Christian Moral Principles* (Chicago: Franciscan Herald Press, 1983), chaps. 35 and 36; Joseph M. Boyle, Jr., "Human Action, Natural Rhythms, and Contraception: A Response to Noonan", *American Journal of Jurisprudence*, 26 (1981): 32–46; John Finnis, "Natural Law and Unnatural Acts", *Heythrop Journal* 11 (1970): 365–87; "*Humanae Vitae*: Its Background and Aftermath", *International Review of Natural Family*

II. CONTRACEPTION: ESSENTIALLY CONTRALIFE

It is clear that the moral act of contraception cannot be defined in terms of any specific pattern of behavior. For there are many different ways to contracept, and there are many outward performances that could, but need not, be ways of contracepting.

On the one hand, the uses of barriers, drugs, and withdrawal are different behaviors often chosen to contracept; they are more-or-less effective. Many people mistakenly rely on contraceptively useless techniques and engage in the behavior such techniques require; any such behavior, too, is chosen to contracept and so morally speaking is a way of contracepting.[5]

On the other hand, outward performances that usually are ways of contracepting can be chosen for other reasons. For instance, to treat some pathological

---

Planning 4 (1980): 141–53; "Personal Integrity, Sexual Morality and Responsible Parenthood", *Rivista di Studi sulla Persona e la Famiglia: Anthropos* 1 (1985): 43–55; William E. May, *Sex, Marriage, and Chastity: Reflections of a Catholic Layman, Spouse, and Parent* (Chicago: Franciscan Herald Press, 1981); *Contraception and Catholicism*, Common Faith Tract No. 5 (Front Royal, Va.: Christendom Publications, 1983); *Contraception, "Humanae Vitae," and Catholic Moral Thought* (Chicago: Franciscan Herald Press, 1984); Ronald Lawler, O.F.M.Cap., Joseph M. Boyle, Jr., William E. May, *Catholic Sexual Ethics: A Summary, Explanation, and Defense* (Huntington, Ind.: Our Sunday Visitor, 1985).

[5] This is why Paul VI in *Humanae vitae*, 14, *AAS* 60 (1968): 490, formulates the rejection of contraception in terms of "any act . . . which intends as an end or a means to impede procreation".

condition, women who never engage in sexual intercourse sometimes have been given drugs usually prescribed for contraception. Fertile married women engaging in sexual intercourse sometimes have taken the same drugs without contracepting, although the therapy had as a side effect that those women could not conceive.

In not being defined by any specific pattern of behavior, contraception is like many other acts, such as apologizing. There are many ways of apologizing, and performances that sometimes count as an apology can have other and even opposite meanings. And in this respect contraception is unlike many other acts, such as shaking hands. To engage in the act of interpersonal communication that we call "shaking hands", one's hand must make contact with the other person's hand.

Sexual acts, such as fornicating, are more like shaking hands than like apologizing. In this respect, sexual acts are unlike contraception. Assuming contraception is a sin, it is not a sexual sin, such as masturbation, fornication, adultery, homosexual behavior, and so on. A dictator who wanted to control population might contracept by having a fertility-reducing additive put in the public water supply. He would engage in no sexual behavior whatsoever and might not will any such behavior. He might also exhort people to abstain but reason that, if they did not, the additive in the water would prevent the coming to be of some of the possible persons he did not want.

Contraception can be defined only in terms of the beliefs, intentions, and choices that render behavior contraceptive. To contracept one must think that (1) some behavior in which someone could engage is likely to cause a new life to begin, and (2) the bringing about of the beginning of new life might be impeded by some other behavior one could perform. One's choice is to perform that other behavior; one's relevant immediate intention (which may be sought for some further purpose) is that the prospective new life not begin. (Here and in what follows, "begin" and "come to be" refer both to the initiation of the life of a possible person and to the continuing existence of the person. Thus contraception aims to impede both the initiation of life and the being of the individual whose life would be initiated if not impeded.)

This definition makes it clear that contraception is only contingently related to marital intercourse. For the definition of contraception neither includes nor entails that one who does it engages in sexual intercourse, much less marital intercourse. Therefore, if someone both engages in a sexual act and contracepts, the two are distinct acts. A young couple tempted to fornicate have two choices to make, not one: whether to fornicate or not, and whether to contracept or not. They may decide to fornicate and not to contracept, perhaps agreeing that if pregnancy occurs they will get married. Many married couples who do choose marital intercourse never contracept; they may be infertile, or no more fertile than they care to be, or ignorant of contraception, or absolutely opposed to it. Thus, those who do choose to contracept plainly do so by a choice and by performances entirely distinct from the choice to engage in marital intercourse and the carrying out of that choice.

Nevertheless, contraception often is thought of as if it were a sexual act, and the morality of contraception treated as an issue of sexual ethics. The reason is that contraception presupposes and is closely related to sexual acts, since there is no occasion to practice contraception unless someone is likely to become pregnant, and pregnancy rarely occurs apart from some sexual act.

Since contraception must be defined by its intention that a prospective new life not begin, every contraceptive act is necessarily contralife. Those who choose such an act often also intend some further good—for example, not to procreate irresponsibly with bad consequences for already existing persons. But in choosing contraception as a means to this further good, they necessarily reject a new life. They imagine that a new person will come to be if that is not prevented, they want that possible person not to be, and they effectively will that he or she never be. That will is a contralife will. Therefore, each and every contraceptive act is necessarily contralife.

Moreover, in and of itself, a contraceptive act is nothing but contralife. For, being separate from any sexual act that occasions it, a contraceptive act cannot be considered part of that sexual act. Thus contraception in marriage is not part of any marital act. Contraception is related to marital acts only instrumentally, inasmuch as contraception lessens the likelihood of pregnancy, which can be a motive to avoid marital intercourse.

This being so, one cannot argue that since marital

intercourse is good, contraception *involved in it* can be acceptable. If the contraceptive act and the marital act were one and the same human act, that argument might succeed, since that one act could be analyzed as an act with two effects. However, the principle of double effect is not correctly used to justify what is done in one act by the good features of another distinct act.

III. CONTRACEPTION: EVIL BECAUSE CONTRALIFE

In reading this section, many will think that our argument proves too much if it proves anything at all, for it will seem to them that NFP does not differ from contraception in any way that would allow NFP to be morally acceptable if our argument concerning contraception is sound. However, rather than attempting to do everything at once, in this section we deal only with contraception and leave until section VI the explanation of how NFP differs in a morally significant way from contraception.

Insofar as contraception is contralife, it is similar to deliberate homicide. If contraception is similar to homicide, the first question is: What is wrong with homicide? In sketching out the answer to this question, we are not concerned with killing that may be justified, such as killing in war, but with the intentional killing of the innocent, which certainly is wrong.[6]

---

[6] For a fuller treatment of the ethics of killing, see John Finnis, Joseph M. Boyle, Jr., and Germain Grisez, *Nuclear Deterrence, Morality and Realism* (Oxford and New York: Oxford University Press, 1987), chap. 11.

Part of the reason why deliberate homicide is wrong is that it is wrong to harm people, and love does no harm. Killing people is an extreme case of harming them. Moreover, in this case the harm to the person is direct and sure, unlike harms that one does to people when—for example, by stealing—one violates certain of their other rights, only indirectly harming the person. One's life is one's very reality. Thus, laying down one's own life for another is the greatest sacrifice one can make.

However, killing someone is not morally wrong only because the person who is killed loses the good of life. If that were the case, it also would be morally wrong to kill anyone by accident, since accidental killing also results in loss of life. An essential condition of the immorality of deliberate homicide is that it involves a contralife will. Although the goodness of the life that is destroyed provides the reason why deliberate killing is wrong, the moral evil of killing primarily is in the killer's heart.

The New Testament makes it abundantly clear, against false, legalistic conceptions, that morality is in the heart. A man can commit adultery without ever touching a woman. And he need not wish to commit adultery with some real woman. Perhaps there is no real woman in the world with whom he wishes to commit adultery. But if he imagines an ideal playmate and freely consents to his wish that she were real so that he might commit adultery with her, he commits adultery. Indeed, any sin is in one's heart before it is in one's deed, and one's sinful deed is wrong because of one's evil heart. Therefore, deliberate homicide is immoral primarily because the contralife will that it involves cannot be a loving heart.

Usually when people contracept, they are interested in sexual intercourse which they think might lead to conception. If they did not think that, they would have no reason to contracept. They look ahead and think about the baby whose life they might initiate. Perhaps for some further good reason, perhaps not, they find the prospect repugnant: "We do not want that possible baby to begin to live." As the very definition of contraception makes clear, that will is contralife; it is a practical (though not necessarily an emotional) hatred of the possible baby they project and reject, just as the will to accept the coming to be of a baby is a practical love of that possible person.

Confusions between feelings and will tend to obscure the moral significance of "desiring", "loving", "wishing", "wanting", "hating", "not wanting", and so on. All these expressions can be used to refer either to emotions or to volitions or to both simultaneously. In very many cases, will and feeling oppose one another, and in very many other cases strong feelings occur quite independently of any relevant willing, and vice versa. Hence, while it may seem shocking to speak of "practical hatred" in referring to the will to contracept, the expression is accurate and must not be misunderstood to suggest emotional animus.

In short, contraception is similar to deliberate homicide, despite their important differences, precisely inasmuch as both involve a contralife *will*. Our thesis is that the contralife will that contraception involves also is morally evil, although we do not claim that it usually is as evil as a homicidal will.

To establish this thesis, we begin with two basic premises that no one is likely to challenge. First, morally right choices must conform to reason and not be contrary to it. Second, in itself the coming to be of a new human person is a great human good. To say this is not to say that this good may not be accompanied by many evils that in the concrete can render realizing it repugnant, but only that, nothing else considered, the prospect of a new person is a reason to act for his or her coming to be and in itself offers no reason to try to prevent that.

Given these two premises, a contraceptive choice certainly cannot be justified if one does not have a reason for making it. (For the moment we set aside the question whether a contraceptive choice can be justified even if one does have a reason for making it.) For the prospective coming to be of the new person offers some reason *not* to choose contraception. So, to choose to contracept without having a reason clearly is to choose contrary to reason, not in harmony with it.

Although some people do choose to contracept without having a reason, they do have an emotional motive. One such motive is that some people find the prospect of the possible person's coming to be unacceptable in itself. Their motivation is like that of murderers who kill someone not for any reason but simply out of emotional hatred. Their attitude clearly is immoral.

The canon *Si aliquis* mentions this motive when it refers to those who contracept out of "hatred".

If those who have this motive did not see a reason not to contracept, they would have no morally significant choice about whether to contracept or not. In particular cases they might be inhibited by aesthetic, economic, or other considerations, including the Church's teaching against contraception. But such inhibitions are accidental to contraception as such, and so we set them aside. Those motivated by emotional hatred of the possible new person, if they lacked any reason to the contrary, would contracept without even considering what for them would not be a possibility: not doing so.

The last point is important not only in the case of emotional hatred but in the other cases to be considered. Choices are made only when some alternative to doing as one chooses—at least the alternative of not choosing—has some appeal. If one has a reason to do something and no motive not to do it, no alternative to doing it has any appeal. In such a case, one has no choice to make and one acts according to the reason without choosing to do so. For example, one notices something that arouses curiosity, thinks of a way of trying to satisfy it, has no motive not to act to do so, and so without having to choose acts to satisfy the curiosity.

However, someone who finds the concrete prospect of the beginning of a new life unacceptable and who thereby is emotionally motivated to reject that possible person's coming to be nevertheless can appreciate the intelligible goodness of a new person's coming to be, see that as a reason not to choose contraception, and yet choose to follow the emotional motive against the reason. Precisely in being thus against reason such a choice to contracept is immoral, and this immorality is not accidental but essential to that choice of contraception.

But few people are motivated to contracept by emotional hatred of the possible person who might otherwise come to be. Generally people have an extrinsic motive. Sometimes the extrinsic motive involves genuine and even very weighty reasons, but sometimes it is merely emotional.

Those who consider the prospect of a new person's coming to be and find that prospect emotionally repugnant, not because of hatred of the possible person but because of other elements of the total prospective situation, might say: "In some ways we would like to have another baby, and we are good parents, but considering everything else we want, we simple don't want to have another baby." (Here and throughout the remainder of this paper, "another baby" should be read to mean "a baby or another baby", and "don't want" should be read to mean "don't want, whether now or never".) Such people can admit that choosing on this basis to practice contraception is contrary to reason and amounts to plain selfishness. But they can be frankly unconcerned about this fact: "We choose to take care of ourselves and don't see anything so wrong with that."

Many people today, especially the affluent, contracept because of such selfishness, whether or not they are fully aware of its immorality. For them moral considerations only become significant when nonrational individual behavior has social consequences. While they freely act contrary to reason when they think it hurts no one other than themselves, their conscience awakens when justice toward others comes into play. Seeing no injustice in contraception, they see no immorality in it. However, serious Christians, and many others as well, reject that mistaken conception of morality. For them the choice to contracept could be justified, if at all, only by some genuine reason.

Reasons vary.[7] For some the reason is that the responsibilities involved in caring for another baby would interfere with career commitments. (Here and throughout this paper, "reason" should be read to mean "reason or set of reasons, however complex".) Others judge that they have their hands full or cannot afford another baby. Those with either of these and various other reasons perhaps rightly judge that having another baby would be morally irresponsible.

Naturally, those who choose for some reason to contracept invoke that reason to justify their action. However, they also know that there is a reason not to contracept, namely, the good of the prospective new person's life, which contraception prevents. (Again,

---

[7] Pius XII, in his Allocution to the Society of Italian Catholic Midwives, *AAS* 43 (1951): 846, provides a list of the kinds of reasons that serve as indications for practicing periodic abstinence: medical, eugenic, economic, and social factors. These same factors provide reasons for those whose choice to contracept is motivated by something more than mere emotional motivation.

we set aside the reasons accidental to contraception that inhibit some from choosing it.) For, if they were simply unaware of contraception's contralife character, they would have no need to make a *choice* of contraception, since they would see no reason not to contracept. (They might well need to make choices *about* contraception, insofar as they might see reasons not to choose certain contraceptive techniques that have bad aspects or side effects.)

If they could choose contraception without choosing contrary to any reason, they could choose it uprightly. But they realize that to contracept is to choose contrary to the beginning of a possible person's life, which in and of itself is a reason to choose not to contracept. Thus, they are aware that they choose contrary to a reason, but they may think that they are not choosing immorally, for they are likely to suppose that their reason to contracept somehow justifies choosing to do so.

However, the mere fact that they have a reason to contracept does not justify their choice to do so. For it does not eliminate the reason not to contracept—the prospective new person's life.

While morality requires that one always act in harmony with reason, it does not—and it cannot—require that one always act on every reason one has for acting. People normally have reasons for doing many more things than they can possibly do. They must choose between or among the things that they have reasons to do. Moreover, immoral choices very often are made not without a reason but for excellent reasons. For example, people often do injustices in order to secure real benefits for those they love. Thus, whenever there is a reason to do something and there is also a reason not to do it, one chooses in harmony with reason by choosing not to do it, but chooses contrary to reason by choosing to do it, unless the reason to do it is *rationally preferable* to the reason not to do it.[8]

Thus, if the choice to contracept is not to be immoral, inasmuch as it is contralife and so far forth contrary to a reason, the reason to contracept must be rationally preferred to the reason not to do so, namely, that in itself the coming to be of a possible person is a great good.

To establish the rational preferability of the reason to choose to contracept, the two reasons must be rationally compared. To do this, one needs a standard by which to compare the two reasons precisely inasmuch as they are reasons for acting. But there is no such standard, nor can there be. (We have argued this point at length elsewhere and will explain it only briefly here.)[9]

---

[8] With respect to the theoretical foundations of the point we make briefly in this paragraph, see Germain Grisez, Joseph Boyle, and John Finnis, "Practical Principles, Moral Truth, and Ultimate Ends", pt. 2, sec. VII, *American Journal of Jurisprudence* 33 (1988), 121–25.

[9] For the full argument against rational commensurability of the instantiations of goods offered by alternatives available for free choice, see Finnis, Boyle, and Grisez, *Nuclear Deterrence*, 249–67, with the notes on 268–72 and the works cited there. The argument against rational commensurability establishes the truth of one proposition signified by saying, "the end does not justify the means". Rational commensurability of goods as reasons for acting would be necessary to justify using a means contrary to one good to achieve

Therefore, the attempted justification inevitably fails, and so the choice to contracept is contrary to reason and therefore is immoral.

If there were a rational method of establishing the rational preferability of the reason *for* making a choice to the reason *against* making it (or vice versa), then the reason that the use of that method showed to be less rationally preferable would, by that very fact, cease to be a reason in respect to that situation of choice. But in that case the situation would cease to be a situation of choice between rationally appealing alternatives, and so there would remain no choice between these alternatives. If the reason for making that choice and the reason against making it were the only motives at work in that situation, one simply would act in accord with the now-unopposed reason. (Of course, there often are other appealing possibilities. Among them can be the option of abandoning reason and following some merely emotional motivation.)

The preceding abstract argument that there can be no rational method by which to establish the rational preferability of the reason to contracept is, we think, conclusive. But many people who acknowledge that it is good to initiate the life of a new person nevertheless think that a choice to contracept can be rational. They

---

an end that instantiates another. "It is not licit to do evils that goods may come about" can express the same proposition. Whether or not it does so in Saint Paul (Rom 3.8) is disputed. It clearly does so in *Humanae vitae*, 14, *AAS* 60 (1968): 491.

are convinced that the competing values must be rationally comparable, somehow or other, since people do in fact compare them.

To do so, people think of and compare two possible futures: One in which the baby lives and one in which it does not. And they think that the future in which the baby does not live is better. It certainly seems so to them. They *feel* that the future without the baby will be better than the future with it. But can they *know* that the future without the baby will be rationally better? Clearly, they cannot. To know that, they would have to know what God knows—not only the immediate, or short-term, or other this-worldly possible futures with and without the baby, but also the place of that possible baby and of everyone else concerned in God's plan for his Kingdom. Human providence does not begin to reach so far.

If the comparison of these two possible futures is not rational, what is it? It is an expression of the feelings of those who make it. The possible future without the baby *seems* better only because that is the future that they want more strongly. Their wanting need not be merely selfish, but it cannot be rational. That the possible future without the baby will be better (something that they cannot know) cannot be what makes them not want the possible future with it. However, their not wanting the possible baby and all the consequences of that baby's coming to be and being can and does make them feel that the possible future without the baby will be better. Therefore, the supposed reason sufficient to establish the rational preferability of contracepting simply is an emotional motive.

Inasmuch as the choice to contracept is contralife and so far forth contrary to a reason, this emotional motive provides no justification at all. The choice to contracept is not only contrary to *a* reason, but contrary to a reason that cannot be rationally outweighed. Therefore, it is contrary to *reason itself*, and so it is immoral.

But do not people who make rational judgments to do this rather than that sometimes begin by comparing possible futures and considering which will be better: the future to be expected if they do this or the future to be expected if they do that? Yes, in two kinds of cases people do compare possible futures as the basis or part of the basis for making rational judgments to do this rather than that.

1. In one set of cases, such a comparison does establish the rational preferability of a certain reason for acting. But by doing so, it eliminates the alternative consideration as a reason for acting otherwise (or for not acting at all). Unopposed, the rationally preferable reason for acting leads of itself to action, and choice is precluded.

For example, if a pilot of a plane about to crash thinks that he can come down in either a more densely or a less densely populated area (and he sees no other difference between the two), his comparison of possible futures establishes the rational preferability, in terms of saving human lives, of steering toward the less densely populated area. But with this rational preferability established (and assuming no other motive is at work), the pilot will have no reason to steer his plane toward the more densely populated area. Thus, choice will be unnecessary, and so the rational preferability—of endangering fewer lives—established by the comparison of possible futures will preclude choice and lead of itself to action, rather than provide a reason for choosing to come down in the less, rather than the more, densely populated area.

One sometimes embarks on deliberation, assuming a choice will be necessary, but discovers that presupposed standards of evaluation and limits on the possibilities to be considered make it easy to establish the rational preferability of one possible course of action and so eliminate the need for choice. For instance, if one is house hunting and is concerned with only three factors—say, price, size, and proximity to school—one may find houses that are better than others in one or two of these respects, but not in all three; none of the reasons for purchasing any of these houses can be judged rationally preferable to the reasons favoring the alternatives. But if one finds a house that is cheaper, bigger, and closer to school than any other house on the market, the rational preferability of the reason to buy it will be established. Moreover, unless one then becomes interested in some additional factor—for example, the character of the neighborhood or the soundness of the structure—one will no longer have any reason to choose to buy any of the other available houses. And thus one will have so unchallenged a reason to buy *this* house that no choice of it will be necessary.

Rational judgments in the technical sphere—judgments of the most efficient means to reach definite ends—typically are made in this way. But moral judgments regarding free choices always concern what is truly good for human persons, and no one can make in a technical way rational comparisons concerning what is truly good for persons as such. Such comparisons are out of reach, because persons are open-ended, and any person is more than the particular goal of any and every human action.

2. In the other set of cases, possible futures are compared, and their comparison does not preclude choice, but neither does it establish the rational preferability of a certain reason for acting. Instead, it contributes in some other way to the rational appraisal of the alternatives between which a choice remains to be made.

For example, one thinking of doing something that will have side effects harmful to others can assess the seriousness of those side effects by asking: "How would I feel if these side effects were impinging on people for whom I cared?" In answering the question, possible futures are compared, not rationally but on the scale of one's feelings. To the subjective appraisal of the significance of the side effects, one can apply the Golden Rule and so reach a moral judgment, for if one's feelings would preclude one's doing the same thing to people for whom one cared, one can judge that the unfairness of accepting the harmful side effects is a good reason not to accept them. Yet one can be tempted—that is, see a reason—to act contrary to that judgment, for one's comparison of possible futures does not establish the rational preferability *in every respect* of the future in which one forgoes acting to the future in which one acts and unfairly accepts the side effects harmful to others.

In neither the first nor the second kinds of cases does the comparison of possible futures establish the rational preferability of the reason for making a choice to the reason against making it (or vice versa). Therefore, these ways in which people do compare possible futures in making rational judgments to do this rather than that cannot be used to show that the reason for making a choice—such as the choice to contracept—is rationally preferable to the reason against making that choice.

Finally, what about those cases in which the couple's reason for choosing to contracept is that they judge that it would be morally wrong for them to have another baby? Certainly there are cases of this sort, and they constitute the most plausible argument to justify the choice to contracept.

But the earlier argument that showed that there can be no rational method for comparing reasons for and against making a choice applies whether or not both of the alternatives are supported by moral considerations. So, the reason that makes it morally irresponsible for some couples to have another baby is not rationally comparable with the reason that makes it morally wrong for anyone to contracept. To choose contrary to either reason is to choose contrary to reason, not in harmony with it, and so is immoral.

Does it follow that such couples are in genuine perplexity, forced to do evil whether they choose to contracept or not? No. Since contraception is one act and marital intercourse another, they can escape this perplexity by abstaining from marital intercourse. In doing that, they can avoid choosing to contracept and so avoid the contralife will contraception involves and also faithfully serve the values underlying their moral obligation not to have another baby. They can act in complete harmony with reason and in no way act contrary to it.

However, it may be objected, marital intercourse, inasmuch as it serves marital love, can be good even if it is certain to be sterile (during pregnancy, after menopause, and so on). Abstinence prevents intercourse from serving marital love. Therefore, some argue that some couples are obliged to practice contraception for the sake of their marital love. If so, the choice to abstain, too, is contrary to a reason. They conclude that married couples who have a moral obligation not to have another baby cannot escape perplexity unless the choice to contracept somehow is in accord with reason in that situation.

How might the choice to contracept not be against reason in that situation? Only if there is, after all, a rational method for comparing the reasons for and against making a free choice. But we have briefly indicated why there can be no such method.

Yet someone will object that in *this* case free choice must be compatible with rational comparison of reasons. For couples certainly do choose to contracept in this situation. And, it will be argued, the reasons also are clearly commensurable: The service to both love and life rendered by contraception is a better reason than the disservice to life involved in it, since love and life are a whole of which life is only a part, and, as everyone knows, the whole is greater than its part.

The answer to this objection is that the prospective new baby's life, which the use of contraception would be chosen to prevent, is not part of the total set of goods—pertaining to both life and love—to be served by that possible baby's not coming to be. The value of the possible person whose life a contraceptive choice seeks to prevent remains rationally incomparable with the value of the possible benefits to love and life that the argument claims can be achieved only by contraceptively facilitated marital intercourse. Thus, the reasons for choosing not to abstain and not to contracept remain rationally incomparable.

We shall explain in section V why the choice to abstain from marital intercourse by a couple who ought to avoid another baby is not really against reason, and in section VI how the choice to abstain can be put into practice with the help of NFP without the nonrational contralife will that contraception essentially involves. But before dealing with these matters, we shall reply to objections that call into question the seriousness of the reason that prospective new life provides for not using contraception to prevent it.

IV. ANSWERS TO OBJECTIONS

Insofar as the preceding argument depends upon taking seriously the life to be of a possible person and likens preventing it to homicide, those who defend contraception's moral acceptability will point to disanalogies. The validity of the argument we have given does not depend on establishing the analogy with homicide. Still, it is appropriate to answer the objections to the analogy, since it both is part of the Tradition we are trying to clarify and makes manifest the gravity of the choice to use contraception—gravity to which the Tradition also attests.

Objection: Contraception does not attack a real person; it only prevents a merely possible person from coming to be. So the contralife will that contraception involves is not homicidal.

Answer: We do not say that the contralife will essential to contraception is homicidal. Still, it is contralife and more like homicide than one might at first suppose. All human acts affect only the future. Homicide does not destroy the victim's entire life; the past and present are beyond harm. Homicide only prevents the victim from having a future. So the homicidal will, like the contraceptive will, is only against life that would be, not against life that is.

Objection: But when people are killed, and their futures cut off, those people are wronged. For they did exist and were deprived of the lives they had. Contraception, however, does not cut off the life it prevents. There is not yet a person to be wronged. Therefore, contraception does no injustice. In this respect, it is very different from homicide, which plainly does the victim a great injustice. Therefore, contraception can be morally acceptable although homicide is not.

Answer: It is true that contraception does no injustice

to the possible person whose life it prevents. But it does not follow that contraception is morally acceptable. For homicide is wrong not only because it involves an injustice but also because it carries out a nonrationally grounded, contralife will—a will that the one killed not be. That is why deliberate suicide is wrong, even on the assumption that it does no injustice to others. Thus, even if contraception does no injustice to anyone, it is wrong because it necessarily involves a nonrationally grounded, contralife will—the same sort of will that also is essential to the wrongness of deliberate suicide and homicide in general.

Moreover, the fact that contraception does no injustice to the possible person whose life it prevents does not mean that one who chooses to contracept does no injustice. For there are two ways in which those who choose to contracept can be acting unjustly.

First, every method of contraception, even sterilization, has a failure rate. When the attempt at contraception does not succeed, an unwanted baby comes to be. Today, aborting the baby is likely to be considered. But perhaps the baby will be accepted and loved. Even so, the baby began life as an accident, as someone unwanted. Choosing contraception with the knowledge that it might fail and a baby come to be *as unwanted* is being willing to put another in a position in which no reasonable person would wish to be. Therefore, choosing contraception is an injustice, even if it succeeds and the harm remains in one's heart.

Second, some of the most effective and widely used methods of birth control—the various kinds of pills and intrauterine devices (IUDs)—sometimes have their effect *after* conception has taken place, by preventing the implantation and/or development of the early embryo. In such cases, birth control is achieved by very early abortion. That is not contraception but homicide. Thus, those who choose such methods of "contraception" do the precise injustice of homicide, even if through ignorance they are not guilty of it.

Objection: But those who believe abortion is wrong might consider these problems carefully, decide to use some form of contraception which they are sure is not abortifacient, realize they are running some risk of conception, but make up their minds at the outset to accept any baby they conceive by accident. Such people avoid doing any injustice, and their wills are not contralife.

Answer: Their wills certainly are not contralife to the same extent as the wills of those who do not care whether or not their method of birth control is abortifacient and/or who never commit themselves to accept babies conceived by accident. But they still want the possible baby whose life they seek to prevent not to begin to be. If a conception occurs, they may keep their good resolution, accept the baby, and not even consider aborting it. But the baby who came to be by accident still would begin life precisely as an *unwanted* person.

Objection: The claim that very early abortion is homicide assumes that the new individual is a person from conception. But nobody can be certain of that. Even Saint Thomas thought that the individual at first is subpersonal, and that a personal soul is infused only some weeks after pregnancy begins.[10]

Answer: Saint Thomas was working with the biology of his time, which was in error in supposing that new living individuals come to be from nonliving material. (That is how it seems if one has no microscope to look more closely.) He was aware, of course, that whatever persons are, they are alive, not nonliving material. So, Saint Thomas had to suppose that the personal soul is infused at some time after the beginning of pregnancy. Today, we know that new living human individuals come to be from living bits of the bodies of their parents. We know that at conception there is a new living human individual, and everything we observe shows that the very same individual (unless death intervenes) lives and develops continuously until birth—and on until death.

On some occasions, the new individual splits into two or more—identical twins, triplets, and so on. Perhaps, on rarer occasions, two or more individuals combine into one. Nonetheless, from conception

---

[10] For a more extensive answer to this objection than we offer here, see the excellent analysis by T. V. Daly, S.J., "The Status of Embryonic Human Life: A Crucial Issue in Genetic Counselling", *Health Care Priorities in Australia: Proceedings of the 1985 Annual Conference on Bioethics*, ed. Nicholas Tonti-Filippini (Melbourne: St. Vincent's Bioethics Centre, 1985), 45–57. Also see Germain Grisez, *Abortion: The Myths, the Realities, and the Arguments* (New York: Corpus, 1970), 25–27; Germain Grisez and Joseph M. Boyle, Jr., *Life and Death with Liberty and Justice: A Contribution to the Euthanasia Debate* (Notre Dame, Ind.: University of Notre Dame Press, 1979), 229–41.

onward, there is nothing but a living human individual or individuals.

But, except in arguments about the status of the unborn and those who will never or never again be able to function in specifically personal ways, everyone today equates "living human individual" with "human person". Of course, some will insist on the logical-metaphysical possibility—which we admittedly have no argument to exclude—that an unborn human individual at some early stage is not yet a person or that the others are no longer persons. That possibility, however, provides no ground for judging beyond all reasonable doubt that living human individuals in either of those conditions are not persons. If there were no motive to kill or otherwise gravely harm them (for example, by experimenting upon them or using their organs), no question about their personhood would be raised.

Therefore, to judge that they are not persons on the basis of the mere possibility that they are not persons is to license killing or harming them *even if they are persons*. The choice to make that judgment against the unborn at some early stage or those who will never or never again be able to function in specifically personal ways is not only a contralife but a homicidal will.

Objection: In practice, contraception may involve injustice. But according to the argument that likens it to homicide, that injustice is not the basic reason why contraception is wrong. The basic reason is that it involves a nonrationally grounded, contralife will, similar to the will involved in suicide. But an important difference remains, for when someone commits suicide, that existing person's life is destroyed. When people contracept successfully, a merely possible person's life is prevented. That difference remains important even if contraception and suicide are alike in some ways.

Answer: Granted, contraception differs from suicide. A possible person is not an existing person. But this difference is not such that, while suicide is wrong, contraception is morally acceptable. For the difference between contraception and suicide does not take away their similarity. Both involve a nonrationally grounded, contralife will.

Moreover, the possible person whose life is prevented is no mere abstraction but an absolutely unique and unrepeatable individual who would exist if he or she were welcomed rather than prevented. For each one of us, merely being allowed to come into existence was a great gift. The beginning of our lives, which contraception perhaps could have prevented but did not, is continuous with the life by which we are now alive. One must bear this fact in mind when one says that contraception only prevents a possible person.

Also, the similarity between suicide and contraception is closer than at first appears. Whenever a baby comes to be from a couple's one-flesh communion, the new person is, as it were, an emerging part of his or her parents. Although contraception intervenes before any new person emerges, it is still a choice to interfere with existing human life. For, in preventing the baby they project and reject, those who choose to contracept attack their own lives as they tend to become one through their sexual act. By contracepting, they commit limited suicide, as it were—they choose to cut off their human life as they are about to hand it on, precisely at the point at which the new person would emerge.

People who do not believe in an afterlife and a provident God generally deny that there can be anything wrong with deliberate suicide, provided that no injustice is done to others. Christians generally are acutely aware of the wrong of deliberate suicide, because they think of what God had in mind for the person who knowingly and freely commits suicide and how he may view that person's self-destructive act.

But is contraception really so different? The projected and unwanted person is envisaged as a real possibility. No one can know what God has in mind for that possible person's life and how he may view those who prevent it. If, as has now been argued, contraception is wrong because it necessarily involves a nonrationally grounded, contralife will, that wrong is aggravated by the irreverence of this will toward God, the Lord of life, with whom human beings can only cooperate, or refuse to cooperate, in responsibly procreating new persons for his Kingdom.[11]

---

[11] John Paul II, Address to Participants in a Study Seminar on "Responsible Parenthood", Sept. 17, 1983; *Insegnamenti di Giovanni Paolo II*, vol. 6, pt. 2 (Rome: Libreria Editrice Vaticana, 1983), 562; *L'Osservatore Romano*, Eng. ed., Oct. 10, 1983, 7, points out that each person comes into existence through God's personal creative love and that married couples only share in God's work, and adds:

A final objection: If contraception is always wrong because it involves a nonrationally grounded, contralife will, is it not wrong to try to prevent a conception that otherwise might follow from rape? Those who do this also project and reject the baby who might come to be.

Answer: One choosing to prevent a conception that might follow from rape could be choosing to contracept. Plainly, this is so when an administrator of an institution housing men and women incapable of giving consent to sexual intercourse makes little or no effort to prevent their copulation but supplies contraceptives to prevent pregnancies. However, rape is the imposition of intimate, bodily union upon someone without her or his consent, and the one who undergoes rape has the right to resist so far as possible. No one doubts that someone who cannot prevent the initiation of this intimacy is morally justified in resisting its continuation—for example, that a woman who awakes and finds herself being raped need not permit her attacker to ejaculate in her vagina if she can force him

---

"When, therefore, through contraception, married couples remove from the exercise of their conjugal sexuality its potential procreative capacity, they claim a power which belongs solely to God: the power to decide *in a final analysis* the coming into existence of a human person. They assume the qualification not of being cooperators in God's creative power, but the ultimate depositaries of the source of human life. In this perspective, contraception is to be judged objectively so profoundly unlawful as never to be, for any reason, justified. To think or to say the contrary is equal to maintaining that in human life situations may arise in which it is lawful not to recognize God as God."

to withdraw. On the same basis, without ever projecting and rejecting the baby who might be conceived, women who are victims of rape (or those trying to help them) who cannot prevent the rapist from ejaculating close to or in the victim's vagina are morally justified in trying to prevent the ultimate completion—namely, conception itself—of the wrongful intimate bodily union.

The measures that are taken in this case are a defense of the woman's ovum (insofar as it is a part of her person) against the rapist's sperm (insofar as they are parts of his person). By contrast, if the intimate, bodily union of intercourse is not imposed on the woman but sought or willingly permitted, neither she nor anyone who permits the union is conceptually able to defend against it. Hence, rape apart, any contraceptive measures must be chosen to prevent conception not insofar as it is the ultimate completion of intimate bodily union but insofar as it is the initiation of a new and unwanted person.

V. MARITAL INTERCOURSE: NOT OBLIGATORY

We considered the argument that, because marital intercourse is necessary to serve marital love, couples whose reason to avoid having another baby is morally grounded are justified in using contraception. We showed that, even granting the assumption that marital intercourse is necessary to safeguard and promote marital love, the use of contraception is not justified. But we promised to show that marital intercourse is not necessary to serve marital love. In now showing this, we shall also clarify the concept of chastity, especially marital chastity.

One must frankly admit that sexual abstinence can have the bad effects often attributed to it. Vatican II teaches: "Where the intimacy of married life is broken off, it is not rare for its faithfulness to be imperiled and its quality of fruitfulness ruined. For then the upbringing of the children and the courage to accept new ones are both endangered."[12] In plain language, the husband and the wife become irritable with one another and express these feelings by treating the children badly. They may be tempted to commit adultery, at least in thought; their love cools; and they are unlikely to welcome another child. The marriage may even end in divorce.

However, these and other bad effects of abstinence from marital intercourse do not follow from abstinence as such. Most married couples sometimes must abstain for reasons other than family planning—necessary separations, illness, and so on. Many people abstain for longer or shorter stretches without becoming irritable, being unfaithful, and so on. In times past many couples abstained for years at a stretch because they judged that they should not have another baby. Many couples today abstain for ten to twenty days each cycle—and sometimes for longer stretches—for the same reason,

[12] *Gaudium et spes*, 51.

and many such couples bear witness to the benefits to their marital relationship of their practice of periodic abstinence.

Couples who abstain from marital intercourse without incurring bad effects are able to do so only because they learn that most of the benefits of their most perfect acts of marital intercourse can be sought and enjoyed in other ways. For example, they can communicate by conversation, gestures, writing notes; they can please one another by giving little gifts, making compliments, planning surprises; they can enjoy being together by playing games, listening to music, going out to dinner; they can express affection by words and touches, even with a certain degree of limited sexual arousal.

What none of this provides, however, is the satisfaction of the sexual urge. Plainly, sexual frustration is the only factor essentially related to intercourse that causes all the bad effects some people suffer due to marital abstinence. This raises the question: Precisely how is the satisfaction of sexual desire related to marital love?

Clearly, marital intercourse is essentially related to marital love. This essential relationship plainly calls for marital intercourse on three kinds of occasions.

1. Marital love begins with the mutual commitment that constitutes marriage and is fulfilled by the marital intercourse that consummates it. That act of sexual intercourse realizes the husband and wife as two in one flesh and provides them with the experience of being married. But this marital intercourse, which serves marital love by consummating marriage, has nothing

to do with the regular dynamics of sexual desire and its possible frustration. A single act of marital intercourse consummates marriage, and that act need not have much to do with sexual desire. As an experience of sexual satisfaction, it may leave much to be desired.

2. Marital love also is fulfilled by marital intercourse on the part of those who desire children and are prepared to welcome them.

3. Of course, there are other occasions—such as anniversaries, special times together, and so on—when marital intercourse is particularly appropriate to recall the significant reality and renew the essential experience—of being one in marital communion—of that marital intercourse that first consummated marital love. However, there is little correlation between the periodicity of spontaneous and undisciplined sexual desire, on the one hand, and the calendar of each married couple's special occasions, on the other.

Someone will object that the calendar of each married couple's special occasions unfortunately also has little correlation with times of infertility. So, the objection will continue, for couples who ought not to have another baby, marital love must remain unserved by marital intercourse on many such occasions unless the use of contraception is justified. Therefore, the objection will conclude, the use of contraception often is necessary quite apart from any urgent need to satisfy sexual desire.

The answer is that marital intercourse is indeed appropriate on such occasions and certainly serves marital love, provided that there is no reason not to engage in it. However, couples who ought to avoid another baby can celebrate such occasions without having marital intercourse, and an important part of their expression and experience of marital love in such cases is their very abstinence from marital intercourse for the sake of the common good—their marital friendship and children—that they are celebrating. Therefore, although marital intercourse would be appropriate, marital love does not require it even for such celebrations.

If anyone thinks such a notion of celebration unreal, that is only because of an underlying assumption that unsatisfied sexual desire would spoil it.

Therefore, while marital intercourse is either required or appropriate on the three preceding kinds of occasions, if one sets aside the factor of urgent sexual desire and its frustration, the requirement that married couples engage in intercourse for the sake of their marital love is very limited. Abstaining from sexual intercourse at times for various good reasons, including the avoidance of pregnancy, is compatible with serving marital love by engaging in intercourse on those occasions when marital love truly requires marital intercourse. And the bad effects of marital abstinence on marital love cannot be attributed to the lack of that marital intercourse that marital love really requires. The bad effects of abstinence—other than those that could be forestalled by appropriate activities not leading to orgasm—are caused by one and only one thing: The urge is there, is powerful, and is not subordinated to the goods of marriage.

True, marital intercourse, even if not required by marital love, often can serve it. A married couple do not need a reason to engage in marital intercourse. Any normal married couple at times desire to engage in marital intercourse and, if there is no reason not to do so, spontaneously act on that desire, often even without deliberating and making any choice. However, a choice always is necessary when they are aware of some reason not to engage in marital intercourse. A couple's moral obligation not to have another baby is a good reason not to engage in marital intercourse.

Still, many people today think that the satisfaction of sexual desire is in itself an important human good, and that one irreducible aspect of marital love simply is the decent satisfaction of this desire within the bounds of marriage. But this widespread view is false for three reasons.

First, in itself the satisfaction of natural desires is not a good of human persons. Desire satisfaction contributes to human goods only insofar as it is integrated within a wider framework determined by reason and morally upright commitments. Such integration is not achieved merely by locating the satisfaction of desires within a context in which it can be legitimate. Rather, integration requires that desire be satisfied only in harmony with all the purposes of the framework within which doing so is legitimate, and that desire not be satisfied whenever satisfying it would conflict with any of those purposes.

Second, the deliberate use of marital intercourse simply to satisfy sexual desire does not serve marital love, because that use of marital intercourse has features that are at odds with marital love itself.

One can see this by considering the question: Does the marital act express and nurture marital love, even if the couple's motive for engaging in it simply is their sexual desire? (1) If they engage in intercourse in response to the urge and contrary to a reason not to engage in it, then it cannot express and nurture love. But (2) if they do not engage in intercourse when there is a reason not to, then, when there is no reason not to, their intercourse motivated simply by sexual desire can express and nurture marital love.

1. Intercourse in response to the urge, engaged in contrary to a reason not to engage in it, cannot express and nurture love, because actions are expressive and communicative precisely insofar as they are free. If a man has an uncontrollable nervous condition such that from time to time he blurts out "Yes, yes!" everyone soon realizes that his "Yes, yes!" is quite meaningless. If his wife wants his agreement about anything important, she asks him to put it in writing. To be able to give oneself in marital intercourse so that it means something, one needs self-control sufficient to be able to choose not to engage in intercourse when there is a reason not to. So, for those who do not abstain when there is some reason not to have intercourse, marital intercourse motivated simply by sexual desire cannot be expressive and communicative of marital love.

Participating in marital intercourse can have the significance of self-giving only if one has sufficient self-possession—one cannot give what one does not have—to be able to resist sexual desire when there is a reason to do so. Therefore, engaging in marital intercourse motivated simply by sexual desire, not habitually shaped by reason, cannot express giving oneself to one's spouse. Rather, it expresses taking one's spouse for oneself. For, in interpersonal relationships, goods received from another that are not truly given are simply taken. In marital intercourse which falls short of mutual self-giving, the taking can be mutual and voluntary, but what is received is not given, only willingly yielded, since the freedom necessary for giving is absent. The couple satisfy one another's desire, but their intercourse does not express and nurture their marital communion as it would if they were free enough to give themselves to one another rather than constrained to take their satisfaction from one another.

2. If couples (for example, during the first months of their marriage) are prepared to practice abstinence when they have a reason not to have marital intercourse—whether that reason is their obligation not to have another baby or some other reason—their acts of marital intercourse are never chosen (despite a contrary reason) simply to satisfy sexual desire. When such couples do engage in marital intercourse, even if sexual desire is their only motive and their behavior is spontaneous rather than deliberate, they can have a genuine experience of their marital communion. As time goes by, their emotions gradually will become integrated; their marital intercourse more and more will come to be fully free and meaningful, less and less mere

spontaneous behavior, and so will conform more perfectly to the ideal of mutual self-giving.

Furthermore, in their acts of abstinence, freely chosen despite their sometimes urgent desire to have intercourse, the couple also realize and experience their marital oneness. For they choose to abstain for a reason, and the reason must be consistent with and can be rooted in their mutual faithfulness to their marital commitment: To be exclusively one with one another in this aspect of their lives, to accept children as a gift, and to fulfill their responsibilities to these children.

There is a *third* reason not to accept the widespread view that sexual satisfaction simply as such can be a reason for choosing to engage in marital intercourse. Because of the importance of this reason, we shall explain it at some length.

Married couples are not alone in experiencing desire and suffering frustration when they do not satisfy it. Very many people have the urge to satisfy sexual desire at regular and rather frequent intervals. So, many children masturbate, many boys and girls engage in sexual play with one another to orgasm, many of those homosexually inclined do what homosexuals do, and many young couples fornicate. When people who have enjoyed such experiences marry, they often continue to engage in sexual activity merely to satisfy sexual desire, even if they limit their sexual activity to marital intercourse. However, being married, they mistakenly think they are justified in satisfying sexual desire whenever they find it agreeable to do so.

But is not the sexual activity of such married couples morally acceptable provided that it is limited to or always culminates in completed marital intercourse? Yes and no. Since they are married, their marital intercourse is appropriate and not wrong as are the ways of satisfying the sexual urge apart from marriage. But if they are not prepared to abstain whenever there is any good reason not to have intercourse, their marital intercourse used merely to satisfy desire remains in that respect like extramarital sexual activity chosen for that purpose, and so is not all it morally should be, as we have shown.

Today, very many people accept the principle that all sexually mature individuals are entitled to regular sexual satisfaction and may get it in any way that pleases them, provided that they do not hurt anyone. Now, what is wrong with this position?

The view that one may satisfy sexual desire simply because doing so is enjoyable and not doing so is frustrating overlooks what such sexual acts do—*do in and of themselves*—to the acting person. The desire-satisfying person becomes the sensory-emotional subject who experiences the urge and its satisfaction; the reasoning and freely choosing subject is disengaged unless put to work in the service of the sensory-emotional subject; and the body becomes an extrinsic object, an instrument for avoiding frustration and replacing urge with satisfaction. The person is dis-integrated. In thus dis-integrating themselves, however, desire-satisfying persons act inconsistently with what they inescapably are: unities of body, sense, emotion, reason, and freedom. The effects of this self-dis-integration of the person are great. For example, communication becomes a problem, since communication is by bodily communion, but persons now are alienated from their own bodies. This self-disintegration is an essential element of what is morally wrong with any sexual activity that is mere desire-satisfaction.

Moreover, engaging in sexual acts simply in response to a sexual urge cuts sexual activity off from its very important relationships with the rest of one's life. Sexual behavior does have something to do with the coming to be of new people. It also has something to do with health and disease. And it has much to do with deep personal relationships. Even masturbators imagine themselves relating to others, and their fantasies affect their relationships with real people. People who merely satisfy their sexual desire with one another are often deeply affected emotionally, yet their shared activity does not really make them one. Each enjoys a private experience and satisfies an urge, but they are not committed to any common good transcendent to their individual selves as a basis for real friendship.

In sum, contrary to what many people today think, the satisfaction of sexual desire in itself is not a human good. Hence, it cannot be an irreducible element of marital love, insofar as marital love is an authentic good of marriage. Sexual behavior motivated by the mere response to sexual desire and the wish to rid oneself of sexual frustration does not become humanly good by the simple fact that it occurs within the framework of marriage. For such sexual behavior is bad for those, married or not, who engage in it. Therefore, sexual desire and its satisfaction by marital intercourse must be subordinated to and integrated with the goods of marriage: The love constituted by the bond of marriage, the communion actualized and experienced in mutual self-giving, and the vocation to serve new life.

Vatican II, in a passage quoted earlier, expresses a clear awareness that breaking off the intimacy of married life can occasion serious harm to both the procreative and the unitive goods. In this section, we have shown that the full service of sexual intimacy to the goods of marriage is compatible with the practice of abstinence when appropriate to avoid pregnancy. Thus, it is clear why the Council does not conclude from the difficulties married couples experience that they are justified in using contraception. Rather, with fidelity to the Church's constant and most firm teaching that contraception is always wrong, Vatican II calls for the practice of chastity. The relevant moral norms, it states, "preserve the full sense of mutual self-giving and procreation in the context of true love. Such a goal cannot be achieved unless the virtue of conjugal chastity is sincerely practiced. Relying on these principles, sons of the Church may not undertake methods of regulating procreation which are found blameworthy by the teaching authority of the Church in its unfolding of the divine law."[13]

---

[13] *Gaudium et spes*, 51; also see *Humanae vitae*, 21, *AAS* 60 (1968): 495–96.

VI. NFP: NOT CONTRALIFE

Ethical considerations apart, NFP can be described roughly but sufficiently for our purpose here as a practice adopted by couples who abstain from sexual intercourse at times when they believe conception is likely and engage in sexual intercourse only at times when they believe conception is unlikely. (The techniques of NFP are equally valuable for increasing the likelihood of conception; couples then choose to engage in marital intercourse when they believe conception is most likely.)

Many argue: How can NFP be chosen without contraceptive intent? Couples using NFP studiously abstain on the "baby days" and have intercourse only during the "safe" periods. It certainly seems that they do not *want* to have another baby and are doing what is necessary to avoid having one. Thus, the argument will go: Those who choose NFP must have exactly the same contralife will as those who choose to contracept. So, the argument will conclude, if contraception really is morally unacceptable, NFP is no less unacceptable.

We concede that NFP can be chosen with contraceptive intent.[14] But we hold that NFP also can be chosen without the contralife will that contraception

---

[14] See John Paul II, General Audience, Sept. 5, 1984; *Insegnamenti di Giovanni Paolo II*, vol. 7, pt. 2 (Rome: Libreria Editrice Vaticana, 1984), 321; *L'Osservatore Romano*, Eng. ed., Sept. 10, 1984, 10; Giovanni Paolo II, *Uomo e Donna lo creò: catechesi sull'amore umano* (Rome: Libreria Editrice Vaticana, 1985), 474.

necessarily involves. To understand the second point, it will help to understand the first.

To see that NFP can be chosen with a contralife will, imagine a married couple who rightly judge that they should not have another baby. But they feel they are entitled to regular satisfaction of their sexual desire and so are not willing to accept long-term abstinence. They choose to use some form of birth prevention. Looking into methods, they find something they do not like about each of them. IUDs and pills can be dangerous to a woman's health. Condoms and diaphragms interfere with the sexual act and pleasure. Jellies and lotions are messy and often ineffective. And so on. Then they hear about NFP. They will have to abstain for a longer stretch than they would like but still will be able to have intercourse during a week to ten days each cycle. Even the abstinence will have its advantages from their point of view: They know it will increase desire and intensify their pleasure. So they decide to use NFP as their method of contraception.

For them, choosing to use NFP is not essentially different from choosing any other method of contraception. They project the coming to be of another baby, want that possible baby not to come to be, and act accordingly. Their will is contralife and no less against reason than if they had chosen some other method of contraception. If pregnancy occurs, the baby will be unwanted.

In our example, the couple rightly judge that they should not have another baby. Of course, couples who have no reason to avoid pregnancy also can choose

NFP with contraceptive intent. But the opposite is not the case: No couple can choose NFP without contraceptive intent unless they have a reason not to have another baby.

Now, if a couple's reason not to have another baby excludes contraceptive intent, that could be so only because their reason does not include the very not-being of the baby. It must include only the burdens that having another baby would impose with respect to other goods, and/or the benefits that might flow from avoiding those burdens.

Thus, the first step in the deliberation and choice that lead to a morally acceptable practice of NFP is to become aware of a reason not to have another baby. Recognizing that intercourse during a fertile time might lead to having another baby, contrary to such a reason, one judges that intercourse during that time is to be avoided. Thus, abstinence is chosen.

This first step plainly is different from a first step toward a choice to contracept based on merely emotional motivations either of hatred of the prospective baby or selfishly not wanting another baby. For here there is a reason.

But the reason not to have another baby when NFP is chosen to avoid the consequences of the possible baby's coming to be might equally well be a reason to choose to use contraception. For a couple who otherwise would welcome another baby might for that very reason choose contraception with a view to preventing the consequences that the couple who choose NFP equally are trying to avoid. How, then, does the practice of NFP differ from the use of contraception in such a case, when the reason not to have another baby is exactly the same?

They differ not in the *reason* for the choices which are motivated, but in the *choices* which that reason motivates and in those choices' relationships to the benefits and burdens which such a reason represents. When contraception is chosen, the choice is to impede the baby's coming to be in order that the goods represented by that reason be realized and/or the evils represented by it be avoided. When NFP is noncontraceptively chosen, the choice is to abstain from intercourse that would be likely to result in both the baby's coming to be and the loss of goods and/or occurrence of evils represented by that same reason in order that the goods represented by that reason be realized or the evils represented by it be avoided.

Even when based on good reasons, the contraceptive choice by its very definition is contralife. It is a choice to prevent the beginning of the life of a possible person. It is a choice *to do something*, with the intent that the baby not be, as a means to a further end: That the good consequences of the baby's not-coming-to-be will be realized and the bad consequences of the baby's coming to be will be prevented. The noncontraceptive choice of NFP differs. It is a choice *not to do something*—namely, not to engage in possibly fertile sexual intercourse—with the intent that the bad consequences of the baby's coming to be will be avoided, and with the *acceptance as side effects* of both the baby's not-coming-to-be and the bad consequences of his or her not-coming-to-be.

In this choice and in the acceptance of its side effects, there need be no contralife will. The baby who might come into being need not be projected and rejected.[15]

In general, those who consider choosing to do something for a certain good but decide *not to do it* in order to avoid bad side effects do not thereby reject the good that they do not pursue. True, not choosing to realize that good—and, indeed, choosing to avoid the burdens one anticipates if one were to realize it—means *not willing* that the good *be realized*, but it does not mean *willing* that the good *not be realized*. In other words: The will's not bearing on the realization of a good is not the same as its bearing on the nonrealization of that good, even if in both cases the will bears on the nonrealization of side effects anticipated if that good were realized.

Not to choose to realize a good—such as the coming to be of a possible person—that offers of itself a reason for its realization can be in harmony with reason. The choice precisely of such a good's nonrealization necessarily is contrary to a reason.

Because the contraceptive choice is contralife, it is in itself contrary to a reason and only seems reasonable insofar as it appears possible to establish that the reason not to have a baby is rationally preferable to the value of the baby's life. But, as we showed, that preferability never can be rationally established.

---

[15] For a fuller treatment than we offer here of the distinction between choosing and accepting the effects of one's choice, see Grisez and Boyle, *Life and Death with Liberty and Justice*, 381–92; Grisez, *Christian Moral Principles*, 233–36, 239–41.

Because the choice of NFP need not be contralife, that choice need not be contrary to a reason. There is a reason to choose to practice NFP: the bad side effects, which one wills to avoid, of having another baby. There also is a reason to choose to go on having intercourse during fertile and infertile times alike: the prospect of having the baby with all the goods associated with that and/or the bad side effects of his or her not coming to be. Whether one chooses the practice of NFP or not, one chooses to act for one reason and does not choose to act for the other, but in both cases one can choose in harmony with both reasons, and need not choose contrary to either. Thus, the choice of NFP need not be immoral. It is merely a case of something common in human life: choosing not to realize something one has a good reason to choose to realize, but whose realization would conflict with avoiding something else one has a good reason to avoid.

Couples who choose to practice NFP do consider what the future will be like if they have another baby. They foresee certain bad effects—for example, they will not be able to fulfill both their present responsibilities and their new ones, and so judge that they should not assume new ones. So they choose to abstain. But they do not have to judge that the possible future without the baby will be rationally preferable to a possible future with it. For their choice to abstain need not be contrary to any reason, and so, assuming it is not, they need not try to justify it by reasoning that their reason for abstinence is rationally preferable to the reason to have another baby—namely, the inherent goodness of a possible person's coming to be.

Apart from the choice to abstain during fertile times, the noncontraceptive practice of NFP involves only two other morally significant elements: the choice to engage in intercourse during infertile times and the choice to adopt a systematic policy of periodic abstinence and intercourse. Neither of these elements need involve a contralife will. The choice to engage in intercourse by those who think they are naturally sterile, permanently or temporarily, cannot involve a contralife will; thinking they are sterile, they cannot choose to do anything whatsoever to impede what they believe to be impossible—the coming to be of a possible person—and so they cannot choose to engage in intercourse with that intent. The adoption of the policy of periodic abstinence could be made to implement a contraceptive choice, as the earlier example showed. But if the adoption of the policy of periodic abstinence does not implement a prior contraceptive choice, the systematization of choices—none of which is contralife in itself—to abstain and to engage in intercourse does not require any additional choice that would be contralife.

Those who defend the morality of contraception will object: The preceding abstract argument simply tries to obscure NFP's obvious moral identity with contraception. It has been admitted, they will point out, that people can have the very same reason for choosing both, and that the reason in some cases can constitute a strict moral obligation not to have another baby. Moreover, in both cases, the purpose is identical: to avoid having that baby. Therefore, they will continue, those who choose NFP and those who choose contraception when NFP would be justified necessarily want the same thing. In either case, the couple do not want to have another baby. And in either case, they will conclude, if pregnancy occurs, the baby is unwanted.

In reply, we agree that there is a sense in which the wanting and the not wanting are the same in both cases. The couples' emotional motivations can be very similar. People practicing NFP often fear pregnancy and, when they think an unexpected pregnancy has occurred, react with acute feelings of sadness toward the prospect of the new baby. They may hope and pray that a menstrual period will come as welcome evidence that no baby is coming. It is fair to say: They do not (emotionally) want that baby. But feelings and wishes are not morally determinative. The wanting that counts morally is willing: choosing, intending, and accepting.

What the abstract argument makes clear is that the willing that relates to the prospective baby's not-coming-to-be is not the same in (1) the choice of NFP with contraceptive intent or any other method of contraception as in (2) the noncontraceptive choice of NFP. In (1) the intention precisely is the will that the possible baby not-come-to-be. Even when their intention that the baby not-come-to-be is for some further end, those who make this choice do *not want the baby*, in the precise sense that, as a means to their further end, they choose the possible baby's not-coming-to-be. But in (2), the noncontraceptive choice of NFP, the choice is to not-cause-the-side-effects-of-the-baby's-coming-to-be by abstaining from causing the baby to come to be. Those who make this choice precisely do *not want to cause the baby*, but they do not choose the baby's not-coming-to-be, although they do accept that not-coming-to-be as a side effect of what they intend.

This fact makes a great difference if pregnancy does occur. Since couples who practice NFP noncontraceptively never will a prospective baby's not-coming-to-be, they do not have to change their will toward the new baby to accept or love him or her. They may find the new baby's coming to be emotionally repugnant, but, whatever their feelings might be, the baby is not unwanted in the sense that counts morally. For, using the word "want" to refer to volitions rather than feelings, the baby does not come to be as unwanted. Thus, there is a real and very important difference between *not wanting to have a baby*, which is common to both (1) and (2) above, and *not wanting the baby* one might *have*, which is true of (1) but not of (2).

Those who agree that there is a morally significant difference between the noncontraceptive practice of NFP and the use of contraception and find the preceding explanation otherwise acceptable might still remain unsatisfied with it as an account of what the Church actually teaches about the difference between NFP and contraception. For, on our account, all that is required to make abstinence noncontraceptive is *a* reason not to have another baby other than one that precisely is or includes the baby's not-coming-to-be. But the Church's teaching is that the upright choice of NFP requires *a serious* reason.[16] Thus, the objection will

[16] Paul VI, *Humanae vitae*, 16, *AAS* 60 (1968): 492: "If, then, there are serious reasons to space out births, which derive from the physical

conclude, the choice to practice NFP is not justified merely by having *some* reason other than the baby's not-coming-to-be to avoid pregnancy.

The answer: Any reason, other than the baby's not-coming-to-be, for not wanting to have a baby is sufficient to distinguish the choice to abstain from the choice to contracept. However, the choice to practice NFP requires more for its justification than that it not be contraceptive. In marrying, Christian couples who do not know they will be sterile undertake to accept parenthood and its responsibilities, for the sake of giving life to new members of the human community and the heavenly Kingdom. If a husband and wife are physically or morally unable to carry out that undertaking, they do not fail morally in not carrying it out. But if they are physically able to carry it out and have no serious reason not to have another baby, yet choose to avoid pregnancy by practicing NFP, they fail morally to fulfill the vocation they accepted in marrying. Therefore, the Church teaches that a serious reason is necessary to choose uprightly to practice NFP. But this teaching is entirely compatible with our analysis according to which a less than serious reason can distinguish NFP from contraception.

The ethics of responsible parenthood is the same as

---

or psychological conditions of the husband and wife, or from external conditions, the Church teaches that it is then licit to take into account the natural periodicity immanent in the generative functions, for the use of marriage in the infecund periods only, and in this way to regulate birth without offending the moral principles which have been recalled earlier."

the ethics of responsible care for the dying. Christian morality requires the same reverence for life in its coming to be as in its passing away. Just as the cherishing of human life in its coming to be does not mean that one always must bring a possible person into being, so the cherishing of human life in its passing away does not mean that one always must keep a dying person in being. Just as abstinence from marital intercourse *can* be justified to avoid side effects of bringing possible persons into being and of their being, so the limitation of medical treatment *can* be justified to avoid side effects of keeping persons alive and of their continuing life. Just as the contralife will involved in the contraceptive choice to prevent another person's coming into being never can be justified by any further end, so the contralife will involved in the choice to bring about someone's death never can be justified by any further end. Just as the reasons for the upright practice of NFP and for the use of contraception can be the same, although in many cases they are not, so the reasons for limiting medical treatment and for euthanasia can be the same, although in many cases they are not. Just as one can choose NFP with contraceptive intent, so one can choose to limit medical treatment with homicidal intent—that is, precisely in order to bring about the patient's death. Finally, just as a reason other than precisely not wanting another baby is sufficient to distinguish the choice of NFP from the choice of contraception, although only a serious reason justifies the former choice, so a reason for limiting medical treatment other than the very ending of the patient's life is sufficient to distinguish nonmurderous letting die from euthanasia, although only a good reason for limiting medical treatment is sufficient to justify abstaining from possible life-prolonging treatment. For, just as a couple, without a contraceptive will, can fail to fulfill their responsibility to give life to possible persons, so those who care for the dying, without a murderous will, can fail to fulfill their responsibility to sustain the lives of actual persons.

Before concluding this section, another important difference between contraception and NFP is worth noting. As the preceding section showed, the choice of contraception, besides being contralife, is inconsistent with marital chastity. Not only is the upright choice of NFP not contralife but it also is conducive to marital chastity and fosters marital love. In using abstinence to avoid having another baby, couples who uprightly choose NFP reject the assumption that they are entitled to regular and frequent satisfaction of their sexual desire. The result is that although they may find ten to twenty days' abstinence during each cycle difficult and frustrating, they do not understand abstinence as some sort of arbitrary imposition.

Moreover, such couples' practice of restraint actually increases their control, and so their freedom, and so the meaningfulness of their marital acts. Their personalities become more integrated rather than self-disintegrated. Their communication improves. And their sense of the dignity of their bodily selves grows.[17]

[17] For an interesting psychological study of the difference between contraception and NFP, see Wanda Poltawska, "The Effect of a

VII. THE INSEPARABLE CONNECTION WILLED BY GOD

Someone who accepts the Church's teaching concerning contraception is likely to observe that even if the preceding argumentation does clarify matters in some ways, not much is gained by it, since the immorality of contraception apart from marriage is not a very important issue, and it is hardly necessary to go to such lengths to establish that the use of contraception in marriage is always wrong. For this follows much more simply and directly from the premise that Pope Paul used: There is "the inseparable connection, willed by God, which man on his own initiative may not break, between the two meanings of the conjugal act: the unitive meaning and the procreative meaning".[18]

Moreover, they will point out, the relationship between the preceding argument and this important truth

---

Contraceptive Attitude on Marriage", *International Review of Natural Family Planning* 4 (1980): 187–206. A sound and useful practical treatment of NFP: John Kippley and Sheila Kippley, *The Art of Natural Family Planning*, 3d ed. (Cincinnati: Couple to Couple League, 1987). (The address of the Couple to Couple League is P.O. Box 111184, Cincinnati, Ohio 45211.)

[18] *Humanae vitae*, 12, *AAS* 60 (1968): 488. By using the words "non licet", the Latin of this passage makes it clear that the connection is inseparable in a morally normative sense. The English translation "inseparable connection . . . unable to be broken" wrongly suggests that the connection is inseparable in some mysterious way, since this translation misses the normative meaning of *non licet* but cannot reasonably be taken to mean that the connection is factually unbreakable.

about the two meanings of the conjugal act remains opaque. Until this relationship is established, the usefulness of the preceding argument to clarify the Church's teaching is at best quite doubtful.

Admittedly, those who believe that the use of contraception in marriage is always wrong find that the inseparable-connection premise illuminates what they believe. And, for such persons, the contralife character of contraception perhaps is clear enough. But we do not think that everyone sees clearly enough that outside marriage, too, contraception is always wrong. And we believe that contraception's use outside marriage ought not to be tacitly accepted, for it remains a great evil and paves the way for the even greater evils of abortion, infanticide, and other attacks on innocent life.

Moreover, nonbelievers and Catholic dissenters almost unanimously deny that the inseparable-connection premise is self-evident or that anything in the Church's teaching has so far established this premise. Thus, they reject as question begging not only the argument of *Humanae vitae* but subsequent arguments using the inseparable-connection premise. Since we are trying in this article to clarify and defend the Church's teaching, it was necessary to proceed without assuming the inseparable-connection premise.

However, the independently established conclusion that contraception is always wrong can serve as a premise to establish the inseparable connection that the Church teaches. Plainly, since contraception is always wrong, one may not break the connection between lovemaking and life giving in marriage by using contraception.

But, of course, one also breaks the connection by engendering new human life apart from marital lovemaking—for example, by in vitro fertilization. Hence, to establish the inseparable-connection proposition, another independent argument is needed against producing babies apart from sexual intercourse. The full statement of that argument would require another article similar to this one, but we offer the following summary.[19]

The proponents of producing babies argue: Desire for the good, the coming to be of a new person, leads to the choice, not wrong in itself, to bring the possible person into being. Granted, it would be preferable, if it were possible, to procreate the baby in the normal way. However, any disadvantage inherent in the generation of babies apart from sexual intercourse clearly is outweighed by the great good of new human lives and the fulfillment of the desire for children of couples who otherwise cannot have them. What can be wrong with this?

The answer: The project of producing a baby precisely is to bring a possible baby into being to satisfy

---

[19] The summary we offer articulates one of the arguments—which we believe stands by itself—proposed by the Congregation for the Doctrine of the Faith, *Donum vitae* (1987), II.B.4–5. For a discussion rather fuller than we offer here: *In Vitro Fertilisation and Public Policy*, Evidence Submitted to the Government Committee of Inquiry into Human Fertilisation and Embryology by the Catholic Bishops' Joint Committee on Bio-Ethical Issues on Behalf of the Catholic Bishops of Great Britain (England: Catholic Information Services, May 1983); William E. May, "'Begotten, Not Made': Further Reflections on the Laboratory Generation of Human Life", *International Review of Natural Family Planning* 10 (1986): 1–22.

the desire to have a baby, and the choice precisely is to *produce a baby*. So, a choice to bring about conception in this fashion inevitably means willing the baby's initial status as a product. Now, this status as a product is subpersonal, and so the choice to produce a baby inevitably is a choice to enter into a relationship with the baby as with something subpersonal. This initial relationship of those who choose to produce babies with the babies they produce is inconsistent with and so impedes the communion of persons endowed with equal dignity, which is appropriate in any relationship among persons.

Of course, those who choose to produce a baby make that choice only insofar as it is a means to an ulterior end. They may well intend that the baby be received in an authentic child-parent relationship, in which he or she will live in the communion that befits those who share personal dignity. If realized, this intended end for the sake of which the choice to produce the baby is made will be good for the baby as well as for the parents. But, even so, because the baby's initial status as a product is subpersonal, the choice to produce the baby is the choice of a bad means to a good end.

Those who participate in producing a baby may only reluctantly choose that the baby be a *product made*. Married couples who seek technical help to produce a baby probably would not choose that the baby come to be with a subpersonal status if they could attain their intended end by accepting a baby as the fruit of marital lovemaking open to new life. But some infertile couples so much want to have a baby that they seek the help of those who produce babies, and both the couples and those who try to satisfy their desires choose to bring babies into being as products, made to order to fulfill a demand.

Just as those who contracept overstep by not wanting babies, those who produce babies overstep by wanting them. In either case, the baby is evaluated, whether as an evil to be prevented or as a good to be produced, by relating the baby's very existence or nonexistence to the desire of someone other than God for a future that excludes or a future that includes that person.

When contraception fails, its contralife character means that the new person comes to be as unwanted volitionally and may well be disposed of by abortion. Similarly, in producing babies, if the product is defective, a new person comes to be *as unwanted*. Thus, those who produce babies not only choose life for some, but—can anyone doubt it?—quietly dispose at least of those who are not developing normally.

Since contraception is always wrong and since producing babies is always wrong, the only morally acceptable way to engage either in lovemaking or in life giving is by engaging in sexual intercourse that is open to new life. Now, what is universally true of both contraception and producing babies is true of them when done in the context of marriage. And God wills that human persons do nothing wrong. Therefore, there is an inseparable connection, established by God, which human persons on their own initiative may not break, between the two meanings of the marital act: the unitive meaning and the procreative meaning.

Those who accept the Church's teaching, however, will hardly be satisfied with this interpretation of the inseparable-connection proposition. They will make a twofold objection.

1. The inseparable connection is more than the mere fact that both contraception and producing babies are immoral. It is a reality immanent in human persons' sexual makeup—part of their God-given nature and sexual functioning.

Answer: There plainly is in human nature and sexual functioning a connection between the procreative and unitive meanings of sexual intercourse. Indeed, in all animals that reproduce sexually the coming to be of new individuals and the union of their parents are naturally inseparable. A copulating pair are biologically a single organism insofar as they function together to hand on their specific kind of life to new individuals. Among human persons, reproduction is human reproduction (the procreation of new persons), and sexual intercourse is human intercourse (an interpersonal relationship). Therefore, for human persons, there is a naturally inseparable connection between the procreative and the unitive meanings of sexual intercourse.

However, this naturally inseparable connection both in lower animals and in human persons is not factually unbreakable by human choices and techniques. Breaking the connection in animals is common and beyond moral challenge, provided that it is done with due regard for the value of animal life and in the interests of human persons. But breaking this connection in human persons—which is equally possible from a technical point of view—is morally wrong. The natural givenness of the connection plainly is not by itself the sufficient reason for this wrongness, since moral norms cannot be derived logically from entirely theoretical premises. However, given that contraception is always wrong and that producing babies is always wrong, the God-given structure of human sexual functioning does establish a connection that human persons may not break between the procreative and unitive meanings of human sexual intercourse.

2. They also will object: The inseparable connection to which the Church's teaching calls attention is in marital acts, not in extramarital, although natural, sex acts such as fornication and adultery without contraception. This inseparable connection follows from the marital act's specific character in such a way that contraception falsifies the truth of the marital act, not merely takes away its life-giving potential.

Answer: The morally inseparable connection between procreation and sexual communion can be fully respected only in marital acts. While natural, extramarital acts of sexual intercourse can respect its life-giving meaning by excluding contraception and while the production of babies need not involve sexual intercourse and so need not violate its lovemaking meaning, only marital acts can actualize the specific communion of two human persons as the procreators of new persons.

To clarify this point, we return to the question: How does marital intercourse express marital love?

Marital love primarily is the bond that is constituted

by the mutual commitment that the couple make when they marry and that they nurture by mutual faithfulness. That bond makes them not simply one flesh but, as it were, one person in respect to that part of life that involves genital acts. Engaging in marital intercourse actualizes their oneness in this respect and enables them to experience it concretely: "We are one, really one, now!" The emotions that accompany this experience are a real and intrinsic part of marital love *only insofar as* they belong to intercourse as a realization of the marital oneness.

Particular married couples may be sterile, and all married couples are sterile at times. Nevertheless, the marriage bond itself establishes the specific type of friendship whose proper common good beyond the friendship itself is the fruit of one-flesh unity, namely, the coming to be, including the nurturing, of new persons. And so the acts that actualize and enable a husband and a wife to experience their unity must be—insofar as it is within their power—the sort of acts that are suited to initiate new life. Therefore, if married couples obtain sexual satisfaction to orgasm by masturbating one another, or by engaging in anal or oral intercourse, or by engaging in contracepted intercourse, they do not engage in marital intercourse. What they do in such cases cannot actualize their marital bond and enable them to experience it.[20]

---

[20] See Elizabeth Anscombe, *Contraception and Chastity* (London: Catholic Truth Society, 1975), for a powerful dialectical argument that contracepted sexual intercourse cannot be a marital act.

Although the emotions they experience may include mutual emotional love, this love will be ambiguous and ambivalent, because it is not essentially related to the real and lasting marriage bond between the couple.

It follows that contraception falsifies the inner truth of conjugal love. The contracepting couple's intimate bodily union—their being two in one flesh—would find in conception a very special completion, because a baby is a unique actualization of a married couple's communion. But in carrying out the contraceptive act, they will to prevent this completion of their communion. In addition to contracepting, they engage in a sexual act, but not one that expresses and allows them to experience fully what they are as a married couple.

Someone will object: But a husband and wife who have intercourse during a sterile period cannot complete their communion by conceiving new life. How do they differ from couples who regretfully contracept because they rightly judge that they should not have another baby? Even if contraception is always wrong, the objection will continue, couples practicing it do not prevent conception *insofar as it would complete their communion*, but only insofar as it would initiate the new life that they should not initiate. So, the objection will conclude, how can their use of contraception falsify the inner truth of their conjugal love?

Answer: The couple who have intercourse during a sterile period cannot actualize and experience their marital unity as fully as they would in fruitful intercourse, but they in no way falsify their oneness. In accepting the nonbeing of the baby as a side effect of abstinence on fertile days, they also accept the side effect of the limitation of their marital communion. But this acceptance is not contrary to their communion. Such a couple are like people who tell less than the whole truth but tell all the truth they can tell and tell no lie.

But the use of contraception, as argued above, necessarily does involve a contralife will. The contracepting couple do not want the baby whose life they might initiate. Yet that baby would be a unique completion of their marital communion. Thus, in positively willing that another child not come to be, they also positively will that their marital communion not be fulfilled in this particular act. Thus, in choosing to contracept, couples also will that their acts of sexual intercourse not be acts of marital communion. They are like people who tell less than they know by telling a lie.

Thus, if marriage is defined, as the Church does define it, as a human friendship whose specifying common good includes the procreation of children, it is logically impossible for a contraceptive act to be a marital act.[21] This is an instance of a general truth: Actions

---

[21] See *Code of Canon Law (1983)*, canon 1055, §1, for the Church's definition of marriage. One need not assert the *primacy* of the procreation of children to assert that it is included in marriage's specifying common good. Thus, *Humanae vitae*, 1, *AAS* 60 (1968): 481, begins by speaking of the married couple's *munus* of transmitting life in cooperation with God the Creator. ("Munus" can be translated "duty", but in this context is more adequately translated "role".) But Paul VI does not rest his reaffirmation of the Church's teaching concerning contraception on an assertion of the *primacy* of the good of procreation, although he equivalently asserts a certain primacy or

directed against a benefit that a certain practice of itself serves cannot logically count as instantiations of that practice. Those who regard a practice as morally good will consider such actions directed against a benefit that specifies it morally evil. But the Church holds as divinely revealed truth that God instituted marriage as a human communion to serve the great good of procreation and that the practice of marriage as God instituted it is morally good. Therefore, the Church validly concludes both that contraceptive acts are not marital acts and that they are immoral.

But this conclusion presupposes a premise that nonbelievers and Catholic dissenters at least implicitly deny: That marriage as the Church defines it is morally good. They propose to redefine marriage in such a way that particular contralife acts within marriage can be marital acts. Since part of what they deny is the Faith's teaching about what marriage is, one can argue effectively against their position on contraception only by independently proving the immorality of contraceptive acts. From the moral wrongness of contraception, the

---

ultimacy of procreation among the finalities of marriage in *Humanae vitae*, 8 (in the sentence beginning "Quocirca"), 485–86. Some claim that Vatican II abandoned the Church's previous teaching concerning the ends of marriage. However, the Council incorporates that teaching by reference (*Gaudium et spes*, 48, n. 1) and also expressly teaches the truth we use as a premise: "By their very nature, the institution of matrimony itself and conjugal love are ordained for the procreation and education of children, and find in them their ultimate crown" (48), and, "Marriage and conjugal love are by their nature ordained toward the begetting and educating of children" (50).

wrongness of their conception of marriage then follows.

When one considers both the logical relationship between contraception and the redefinition of marriage, and the existential connections between the practice of contraception and the perversion of marital love, one can understand why the increase in use of contraception by Catholics since 1960 has resulted neither in happier and more stable marriages nor in more truly responsible parenthood. On the contrary, divorce has increased, the indications are that infidelity has increased, many children and young people are freely engaging in sexual practices that cripple their capacity for meaningful sexual activity in any future marriage, many middle-aged Catholics have had themselves surgically sterilized, and many Catholic couples have aborted one or more of their children.

For anyone who believes traditional Christian teaching concerning marriage itself, a rational argument against contraception, such as we have offered, is hardly necessary for conviction about the truth, but may be helpful to understand the meaning, of the Church's teaching that every marital act ought to be open to new life. The traditional condemnation of contraception was shared by all Christians until very recently. In reaffirming that teaching and calling for continued assent to it, the Popes of the twentieth century have relied upon and invoked the authority of this unbroken Tradition going back to the beginning.

John Paul II also has provided careful analyses of the relevant scriptural data and drawn the conclusion that the moral norm excluding contraception "belongs not only to the natural moral law, but also to the *moral order revealed by God*: also from this point of view, it could not be different, but solely what is handed down by Tradition and the Magisterium".[22] We agree. It is beyond reasonable doubt that the Church's teaching that contraception is always wrong has been infallibly proposed by the ordinary Magisterium. This teaching ought to be accepted by every Catholic as a matter of faith.[23]

VIII. SOME PASTORAL IMPLICATIONS

Among pastors *who accept the Church's teaching* that contraception is always wrong, there are four pastoral approaches to the use of contraception that we believe to be disastrously mistaken.

First, some think that Paul VI and John Paul II have made a tactical mistake by insisting on this teaching. According to this view, although contraception is evil,

---

[22] See John Paul II, General Audience, July 18, 1984; *Insegnamenti di Giovanni Paolo II*, vol. 7, pt. 2 (Rome: Libreria Editrice Vaticana, 1984), 102; *L'Osservatore Romano*, Eng. ed., July 23, 1984, 1; Giovanni Paolo II, *Uomo e Donna lo creò: catechesi sull'amore umano* (Rome: Libreria Editrice Vaticana, 1985), 457.

[23] See John C. Ford, S.J., and Germain Grisez, "Contraception and the Infallibility of the Ordinary Magisterium", *Theological Studies* 39 (1978): 259–61; Grisez, *Christian Moral Principles*, chap. 35; Germain Grisez, "Infallibility and Specific Moral Norms: A Review Discussion" (a reply to Francis A. Sullivan, S.J.), *Thomist* 49 (1985): 248–87.

it is a less serious matter than many others, and it is unfortunate that the Popes have put too much emphasis on what would fall into its proper place if only quietly ignored.

We think that anyone who not only believes that contraception is always wrong but understands why it is wrong can easily see that Paul VI and John Paul II have made no mistake in treating this as a matter of great importance.

The choice to contracept, as we have shown, always involves an unjust will and an objective injustice to every child who comes to be as unwanted. Indeed, this unjust will and status put all unwanted children in peril of their lives. So-called methods of contraception that are actually abortifacient regularly kill the embryonic persons who are conceived while these methods are used.

Moreover, one's free choices, once made, determine one's self unless and until one makes another, incompatible choice. Free choices made by two or more persons in communion determine their interpersonal relationship with one another. Thus, by their free choices persons and groups of persons build themselves up day by day, for good or evil. Those who deliberately make the contralife choice of contraception and maintain that choice have contralife hearts. Married couples who make this choice and maintain it do not merely commit isolated acts of contraception but have hearts that are not marital. Their very relationship with one another, perverted by their contraceptive commitment, is inconsistent with the sacramental bond that unites them.

Rather than sanctifying one another, they slip together toward spiritual self-destruction.

Chaste marital intercourse serves marital love in several ways, all of them compatible with abstinence whenever pregnancy ought to be avoided. So, as we have shown, contraception is necessary not to serve marital love but to facilitate the satisfying of sexual desire insufficiently ordered by the goods of marriage. Precisely insofar as sexual intercourse responds to nonintegrated desire, such intercourse even within marriage lacks the significance of mutual self-giving and so neither expresses nor nurtures marital communion. Moreover, precisely insofar as people choose to satisfy nonintegrated sexual desire, they determine themselves in self-dis-integration.

Plainly, not all who use contraception become involved to the same extent in its dynamism toward interpersonally meaningless and self-dis-integrating sexual behavior. However, to the extent that one does engage in unchaste sexual behavior, whether outside marriage or within it, such behavior has further serious consequences.

Very often, when people habitually engage in meaningless sexual behavior, their sense of what is real becomes distorted: What satisfies or frustrates desire is real ("relevant"), while unseen realities, such as God and heaven, seem less real ("irrelevant"). Moreover, the dignity of the fleshly dimension of the person is denied, and any moral argument that calls attention to it is likely to be dismissed as "biologism". One effect of this attitude on Christians imbued with it is that they find it difficult to take seriously those many aspects of faith that involve bodiliness: Incarnation, resurrection, bodily Presence of Jesus in the Eucharist, Virgin Birth, original sin, and so on. "How could salvation depend so much on the biological?"

Thus, the deliberate choice to contracept not only attacks human life in its beginning, but also damages Christian marital love and personal integration. As a form of unchastity, the practice of engaging in intercourse mutilated by contraception tends to upset the Christian appreciation both of transcendent reality and of bodiliness and so threatens faith and hope themselves. Plainly, Paul VI and John Paul II make no mistake in insisting on the Church's teaching on contraception, and their concern with it is true pastoral wisdom.

The second mistaken pastoral approach to the use of contraception is based on the thought that if a diversity of theological opinions on this matter were tolerated in the Church, the whole problem would be solved. According to this view, while contraception is evil, those who choose this evil in good faith commit no sin, and so leaving them in good faith would eliminate the evil of contraception insofar as it is a significant pastoral concern.

We think that, while it is true that those who practice contraception in good faith—if they truly are in good faith—commit no sin, it is by no means true that a policy of leaving everyone in good faith fulfills pastoral responsibility in this matter.

The choice to contracept, even if it is made in conformity to a sincere conscience, is a contralife will.

Objective injustices remain: To every child who is conceived unwanted and to every embryonic person whose life is snuffed out. The contralife self-determination remains, along with a commitment to nonmarital acts that injures the sacramental marriage relationship. The trivializing of sexual activity remains, and even the danger of unchaste sexual activity to faith and hope. Without personal sin, the contraceptive activity of those left in good faith still involves that activity's objective evils.

Moreover, it is questionable whether all Catholic couples who choose contraception truly are in good faith in regarding it as morally acceptable. Both the essential contralife character of the choice and its immorality certainly are knowable by reason. Moreover, this moral truth is clearly and firmly asserted by the Church, in teaching of which everyone is aware. It is easy to say that one sincerely considers contraception morally acceptable, but it is another matter for moderately well instructed Catholics to be morally certain of that.

What is the condition of those not truly in good faith in choosing contraception? A conscience that is not in good faith in approving any lasting element of one's life is fixed in error through rationalization and self-deception. Those in this condition cannot easily overcome their error. At times their conscience bothers them, but they are hardly likely to become clearly aware that their conscience and their way of life in accord with it are immoral. And so, all who are left in *this* kind of "good faith" in reality are left in obdurate sin, and their repentance, which ought to be encouraged, instead is made less likely.

Therefore, since a pastoral policy of tolerating dissent in order that people may be left in good faith not only ignores or complacently accepts the many objective evils involved in contraception but also imperils the souls of those whom the policy was intended to save, John Paul II and the bishops who stand with him are exercising real pastoral care when they not only insist on the truth of Catholic teaching in this matter but courageously work against dissent rather than tolerate it.

The third mistaken pastoral approach to the use of contraception is based on the thought that pastoral compassion and accommodation can bridge the gap between what the Church teaches about contraception and what the faithful do about it. According to this view, the faithful should be encouraged to accept the Church's teaching as an ideal and to strive by a gradual process to approximate this ideal. But they should not be required, as a condition for receiving absolution, to confess sins of contraception and have a firm purpose of amendment.

We think that any policy of gradualism that encourages the faithful to regard contraception as if it were in practice a venial sin or even a mere imperfection does in its fashion accommodate the moral truth the Church teaches to the widespread practice of contraception. But the accommodation is made at the cost of coherence. For the truth that the Church teaches about the real and serious significance of *practicing* contraception is treated as if one could believe it in theory without taking it seriously in *practice*. Such incoherence is hardly a basis for authentic pastoral compassion.

The faithful encouraged to try by a gradual process to eliminate contraception do not eliminate it at once; meanwhile, they persist in the contraceptive choice. While they strive to approximate what they accept as an ideal, they continue to recognize that they live in sin. Although they act as if contraception were not a grave matter, the natural law written in their hearts and the Church's teaching tell them otherwise. Yet those who try to put gradualism into practice, with the encouragement of trusted pastors who seem faithful to the Church's teaching, could only with great difficulty face up to their sin's seriousness and repent. Thus, the disastrous pastoral mistakes of the first two approaches are combined in a policy of gradualism of this sort.

Furthermore, those misled by the pastoral policy of gradualism internalize their pastors' incoherence. On the one hand, they condemn their own contraceptive acts, but, on the other hand, they have a purpose not of amendment but of indefinite persistence in such acts.

But a will consistent with itself is needed to overcome any sin. The sexual urge is powerful. Those who think that satisfying it will be no more than a venial sin are hardly likely to gain self-control. Thus, their inconsistent will is likely to achieve little or no progress toward virtue.

Still worse, the inconsistency almost certainly will spread to other matters. Under these conditions, the whole of a Christian's life is likely to become an incoherent and unstable amalgam of professed ideals, contrary practices, and duplicity of heart.

Therefore, since the pastoral policy of gradualism that treats contraception as if it were merely a venial sin nurtures pharisaism rather than Christian singleheartedness, Paul VI and John Paul II have been truly compassionate pastors in rejecting this approach. They have urged the faithful to accept the truth about contraception and live by it. At the same time, they have emphasized the correct use of the sacrament of penance and the regular, fruitful reception of the Eucharist as the sources of God's mercy and love, which offer those who truly follow Jesus the power to overcome sin in their lives. They coherently insist: "To diminish in no way the saving teaching of Christ constitutes an eminent form of charity for souls."[24] Their true gradualism envisages "a progress that demands awareness of sin, a sincere commitment to observe the moral law, and the ministry of reconciliation".[25]

---

[24] *Humanae vitae*, 29, *AAS* 60 (1968): 501; *Familiaris consortio*, 33, *AAS* 74 (1982): 121.

[25] John Paul II, *Familiaris consortio*, 34, *AAS* 74 (1982): 124. Summarizing the same teaching, John Paul II, Address to participants in a seminar on "Responsible Parenthood", Sept. 17, 1983; *Insegnamenti di Giovanni Paolo II*, vol. 6, pt. 2 (Rome: Libreria Editrice Vaticana, 1983), 564; *L'Osservatore Romano*, Eng. ed., Oct. 10, 1983, 7, forcefully recalls Catholic teaching concerning grace: "To maintain that situations exist in which it is not, *de facto*, possible for the spouses to be faithful to *all* the requirements of the truth of conjugal love is equivalent to forgetting this event of grace which characterizes the New Covenant: the grace of the Holy Spirit makes possible that which is not possible to man, left solely to his own powers. It is

The fourth mistaken pastoral approach is based on the thought that widespread education in the technique of NFP together with likely improvements in it will eventually eliminate the problem of contraception. According to this view, when married couples need abstain only a few days a month to avoid pregnancy, hardly anyone, believer or unbeliever, will be interested in using any other method.

Obviously, the hope that NFP will solve the pastoral problem is consistent with the truth that the Church teaches: that contraception is wrong and NFP morally acceptable. But we think that NFP as a mere technique will never solve the pastoral problem posed by contraception. For although technique is helpful, the problem is a moral one, and no technique makes the heart good. NFP, as we showed, can be chosen as a method of contraception. A pastoral policy that puts too much faith in the mere technique encourages this wrong choice.

Catholics who choose to contracept but out of fidelity to the Church's teaching adopt NFP as their method are truly in good faith. They choose as they do because they think their choice conforms to the truth that the Church teaches. Furthermore, since they choose to abstain, and abstinence need not mean that one wills that another baby not come to be, they easily overlook the

---

therefore necessary to support the spouses in their spiritual lives, to invite them to resort frequently to the Sacraments of Confession and the Eucharist for a continual return, a permanent conversion to the truth of conjugal love."

contralife character of their underlying intention. Thus they have a contraceptive intention but lack sufficient reflection as to its moral significance. And, more important, they have, and realize the significance of, the intention to live according to the Church's teaching about marriage, the marital act, and its lovemaking and life-giving meanings.

Because their method of contraception cannot harm any embryonic life, what they do cannot lead to the grave objective injustice of supposedly contraceptive methods that in fact are abortifacient. Still, their contralife will entails that unexpected conceptions are unwanted babies, and they might even be tempted to abort them. Yet their fidelity to the Church's teaching will help them to resist this temptation.

Although they do have an underlying contraceptive intention, this intention is carried out only by their choices to abstain. Consequently, their acts of sexual intercourse on days they believe are infertile remain marital in character. Insofar as they are marital, their acts of intercourse can embody true marital love. And, because their dominant intention is to live according to the Church's belief about what marriage is, they are not tempted to try to redefine the very meaning of marriage.

Moreover, the practice of NFP, even when chosen as a method of contraception, does require self-control. This self-control enables couples gradually to gain the freedom necessary for self-giving, so that the meaningfulness of their marital acts as expressions of love can develop. And, because their activity is shaped by their fidelity to the Church's teaching, their increasing self-control is not merely a psychological power but a real Christian virtue. This virtue prevents their sexual activity from leading to their self-dis-integration and so prevents the bad consequences unchastity has for faith and hope.

Thus, this fourth pastoral approach is not so disastrous as the first three. Nevertheless, even it is disastrous, because it fails to teach the faithful the complete moral truth that they need and deprives them of the stability that only truth can give to moral life.

If NFP is chosen, even by Catholics in true good faith, as a method of contraception, it probably will not "work". Choosing NFP in this way leaves untouched the false assumption that people are entitled to regular sexual satisfaction. Those making this assumption are unlikely to find ten to twenty days of abstinence in every cycle acceptable. They will not see that by abstaining they are gaining more meaning and more truly giving themselves to one another than they ever could by responding regularly to their sexual urge. They will be tempted to cut corners, with an unexpected pregnancy the likely result.

In case of pregnancy, those who, even in good faith, choose NFP as a method of contraception will unfortunately be tempted to treat unwanted babies as unwanted. Only knowledge of the truth about new life and consistent willing of that good would enable them to welcome children and cherish them with all the generosity they deserve. Moreover, when unwanted pregnancies occur and the couple decide that NFP does not "work" as they had hoped, they will be strongly tempted to abandon their faithfulness to the Church's teaching and to adopt what they will fully recognize as contraception.

Therefore, since a pastoral policy that relies upon the mere technique of NFP to meet the moral challenge of contraception will provide only a partial and unstable response, John Paul II is profoundly correct in insisting not only on the truth of the Church's teaching on contraception but also on the truth of her teaching about NFP. "The *difference*," he says, "*both anthropological and moral*, between contraception and recourse to the rhythm of the cycle . . . is a difference which is much wider and deeper than is usually thought, one which involves in the final analysis two irreconcilable concepts of the human person and of human sexuality."[26]

---

[26] *Familiaris consortio*, 32, *AAS* 74 (1982): 120.

Contraception and the Infallibility of the Ordinary Magisterium

by

JOHN C. FORD, S.J.

and

GERMAIN GRISEZ

I

In a work published in 1963, one of the present authors and another collaborator considered the question whether the received Catholic teaching on contraception had been proposed infallibly.[1] In summing up theological opinion to 1962, they said the teaching that contraception is intrinsically and gravely immoral is "at least definable doctrine".[2] In using this expression, they did not intend to create a new category between infallibility and noninfallibility.[3] Rather, by the words "at least definable doctrine" they intended to embrace the judgments of various groups of theologians. One group held that Pius XI defined the doctrine *ex cathedra* in *Casti connubii*; a second group held that he only reaffirmed there a teaching already proposed infallibly by the ordinary Magisterium; a third group made

Reprinted with permission from *Theological Studies*, vol. 39, no. 2, June 1978, pp. 258–312.

[1] John C. Ford, S.J., and Gerald Kelly, S.J., *Contemporary Moral Theology*, vol. 2, *Marriage Questions* (Westminster, Md.: Newman, 1964), 263–71.

[2] Ibid., 271.

[3] Charles E. Curran, Robert E. Hunt, and the "Subject Professors", with John F. Hunt and Terrence R. Connelly, *Dissent in and for the Church: Theologians and Humanae vitae* (New York: Sheed & Ward, 1969), 177, misunderstood the intent in this way.

various comments which seemed compatible with the view that the received teaching could be defined.

Like the second group, the collaborators in the 1963 publication judged that the received Catholic teaching on contraception had been infallibly proposed by the ordinary Magisterium. This judgment was based on available evidence indicating that a worldwide survey of Catholic bishops would have shown that they all accepted and taught the received teaching.

In this same study its coauthors pointed out that Pius XI and Pius XII did not propose a new teaching on contraception but repeated a teaching reaching back through the centuries. Even those Anglicans who supported the approval of contraception in 1930 admitted the existence of a long Christian tradition, although they denied the power of this tradition to bind the judgment of Christians today. The coauthors argued that one could show that the tradition is normative for Catholics by considering the implications of the fact that during the last century and one half—from 1816 to 1962—the Catholic Church constantly and emphatically taught that contraceptive acts are objectively grave violations of the law of God.

> For, if the teaching of the Catholic Church on a point so profoundly and intimately connected with the salvation of millions of souls has been the same over such a long period of time, the inevitable conclusion must be that that teaching is true and unchangeable. Otherwise the Church which God has established to interpret the moral law and to guide souls on the way

of salvation would be failing substantially in its divine mission.[4]

The collaborators in the 1963 publication did not clarify the relationship between this consideration—which bears upon the binding force of *the Tradition* of Catholic teaching on contraception—and the infallibility with which they believed the ordinary Magisterium *was proposing* the same teaching *in 1962*, when they were completing this work.

In the present article we argue that the received Catholic teaching on contraception has been proposed infallibly by the ordinary Magisterium. The argument we now advance is intended to develop and complete the argument quoted above for the binding force of the Tradition. Vatican Council II has articulated the conditions which must be met for the ordinary Magisterium of the bishops dispersed throughout the world to proclaim the teaching of Christ infallibly. We shall try to show that in the course of the Tradition these conditions have been met. If these conditions have been met, then the reason why the Tradition is binding is clear: a divinely guaranteed teaching is involved. Such teachings, once given, cannot later be contradicted by the Church as a whole. Of course, such teachings and even defined doctrines are open to development by the Church and can be contradicted by the erroneous opinions of members of the Church, including members of the Magisterium.

[4] Ford and Kelly, *Contemporary Moral Theology*, 2:258.

The argument we shall advance here has implications beyond the particular matter—the teaching on contraception—with which we are going to deal. Many received teachings in matters of faith and of morals are being questioned or denied today, and the possibility often is ignored that these teachings might have been proposed infallibly even if they have not been defined. We hope that our present essay will draw attention to this possibility, which ought to be taken into account whenever the status of any received teaching is discussed.

The possibility that the received Catholic teaching on the morality of contraception has been proposed infallibly by the ordinary Magisterium was generally ignored in the debate which took place after the publication of *Humanae vitae*. Everyone agreed that Paul VI proposed no *ex cathedra* definition, and the supposition that Pius XI might have proposed such a definition in *Casti connubii* was hardly mentioned in the debate. Thus those who dissented from the teaching reaffirmed in *Humanae vitae* and those who defended the legitimacy of such dissent proceeded directly from the nondefinitive character of Paul VI's pronouncement to the possibility of licit dissent from noninfallible teachings, ignoring the possibility that the nondefinitive pronouncement contained a reaffirmation of a teaching which, even if never defined, was already infallibly proposed by the ordinary Magisterium.[5] Those who sup-

[5] See, e.g., Curran, Hunt *et al.*, *Dissent*, 25–26, 63. An influential article—not dissenting but considering the possibility of doing so licitly—which exemplifies the same oversight is Karl Rahner, S.J., "Zur

ported the teaching reaffirmed in *Humanae vitae* and who questioned the legitimacy of dissent from it similarly argued that the teaching should be accepted as authoritative and binding, even if noninfallible.⁶ As

---

Enzyklika 'Humanae vitae'", originally published in *Stimmen der Zeit* 93 (1968) and widely republished in translation, e.g., "On the Encyclical 'Humanae vitae'", *Catholic Mind* 66 (Nov. 1968): 28–45; Rahner goes directly from the nondefinitive character of the *document* to a discussion of the reformability and therefore the possible falsity of the *teaching*. Richard A. McCormick, S.J., "Notes on Moral Theology: January–June, 1968", *TS* 29 (1968): 707–41, extends his coverage to include *Humanae vitae* and certain reactions to it; he assumes throughout that infallibility is not in question. In discussing relevant ecclesiological questions, Gustav Thils, "II, 'Sentire cum ecclesia'", in *Pour relire* Humanae vitae: *Déclarations épiscopales du monde entier* (Gembloux: Duculot, 1970), 15*–22*, treats the infallibility of the extraordinary Magisterium *in defining* and the infallibility of the whole Church *in believing*, but neglects to consider the infallibility of the ordinary Magisterium (under certain conditions) *in teaching*.

⁶ E.g., Austin Vaughan, "Msgr. Vaughan Answers Critics", *National Catholic Reporter*, Sept. 11, 1968, states such a case well and briefly; James J. Mulligan, *The Pope and the Theologians* (Emmitsburg, Md.: Mt. St. Mary's, 1968), 13–88, more fully develops this approach. Even those who suggested explicitly that the teaching on contraception might be infallible did not usually develop the argument by applying to the data of history the criteria for the infallible exercise of the ordinary Magisterium articulated by Vatican II. See, e.g., Archdiocese of Washington, *Sex in Marriage: Love-giving, Life-giving* (Washington, D.C.: 1968), 4–5; Joseph F. Costanzo, S.J., "Papal Magisterium and 'Humanae vitae'", *Thought* 44 (1969): 377–412, esp. 410, n. 9. But the argument was proposed, very briefly, by Marcelino Zalba, S.J., *La regulación de la natalidad* (Madrid: B.A.C., 1968), 133–40; "Applicatio encyclicae 'Humanae vitae' apud conferentias episcopales", *Periodica de re morali, canonica, liturgica* 59 (1970): 390; *Las conferencias episcopales ante la* Humanae vitae *(Presen-*

evidence of the obligatory character of the teaching, they frequently cited Vatican II, *Lumen gentium* 25, regarding the religious allegiance of will and of intellect due authentic teaching of the bishops and especially of the Pope, even when the infallible exercise of the Magisterium is not in question.[7]

To a great extent, the debate which took place after the publication of *Humanae vitae* was conducted within a framework established by the statements of Msgr. Ferdinando Lambruschini at the press conference at which *Humanae vitae* was released. Lambruschini's formal statement made clear that the encyclical contained no *ex cathedra* pronouncement and also seemed to rule out the possibility that it was a reaffirmation of a teaching already infallibly proposed; his reported answers to questions raised by reporters at the conference indicated that Lambruschini thought that contraception might eventually be accepted by the Church.[8]

---

tación y comentario) (Madrid: Editorial Cio, 1971), 63–65, 93, 124–26, 130–32, 179; Zalba's writings since 1967 have been hardly noticed in the English-speaking world.

[7] Curran, Hunt, *et al.*, *Dissent* 113, suggest that Paul VI himself, in *Humanae vitae*, 28, specified the assent he expected as that to an authoritative but noninfallible teaching. However, the official text of *Humanae vitae* (*AAS* 60 [1968]: 481–503) refers (501, n. 39) to the *whole* of *Lumen gentium*, 25: "*AAS* 57 (1965): 29–31". Moreover, n. 39 is placed in *Humanae vitae*, 28, to include a reference to Vatican II's teaching on the light of the Spirit, which is mentioned in *Lumen gentium*, 25, especially in respect to *infallible* teachings.

[8] "Press Conference on Encyclical 'Humanae vitae' ", *L'Osservatore Romano*, Eng. ed., Aug, 8, 1968; Associated Press report, published in the *Washington Evening Star* (Washington, D.C.), July 29, 1968;

The framework for response to *Humanae vitae* established by Lambruschini's remarks was readily adopted in the climate of opinion that had developed between 1964 and 1968. Because of the widespread controversy over the morality of contraception which unfolded within the Catholic Church and because of the prolonged study to which Pope Paul himself subjected certain questions related to this topic, many people assumed that the substance of the received Catholic teaching on contraception was itself in doubt and that the eventual papal statement might change it. Even those who denied that the received teaching was in doubt rested their case on the authority of contemporary papal statements and of the teaching of Vatican II in *Gaudium et spes* 51, with its famous footnote 14.[9] Thus, between 1964 and 1968 attention was diverted from the weight of the Tradition of Catholic teaching on the morality of contraception and directed toward the expected papal reply to the questions which were raised in the course of the controversy.

Meanwhile, Vatican II in *Lumen gentium* 25 reaffirmed the possibility of infallibility in the exercise of the ordinary Magisterium and articulated, more clearly than in any previous authoritative document, the conditions under which the bishops dispersed throughout the world proclaim the teaching of Christ

---

the same and similar reports were widely disseminated in all the media the same evening and the following morning.

[9] See, e.g., John C. Ford, S.J., and John J. Lynch, S.J., "Contraception: A Matter of Practical Doubt?" *Homiletic and Pastoral Review* 68 (1968): 563–74.

infallibly. Moreover, the controversy over contraception stimulated historical studies which added much to previous knowledge about the Tradition of Catholic teaching on this matter. But no one—so far as we know—applied the conditions for infallibility in the exercise of the ordinary Magisterium to the facts of the Tradition of Catholic teaching on contraception, and thus no one advanced the argument we are about to propose. Since no one advanced the argument, neither did anyone reply to an argument which clearly and fully put forward the case for the thesis that the received Catholic teaching on the morality of contraception has been proposed infallibly by the ordinary Magisterium.[10]

Clearly, if this thesis is correct, the significance and legitimacy of many reactions against *Humanae vitae* should be reevaluated. Thus the thesis we are about to defend is important; it at least deserves careful examination.

In the present article we prescind from several issues, and we make certain assumptions. First, we prescind from the question whether the moral norm excluding contraception is divinely revealed. Second, we prescind from the question whether Pius XI made an *ex cathedra* definition in *Casti connubii*. Third, we prescind from the question of the extent and limits of the obligation to give religious allegiance of the will and of the intellect

---

[10] In section V we shall show how it happened that neither in the papal Commission before *Humanae vitae* nor in the debate on Hans Küng's book on infallibility afterward was the argument we are about to present articulated and criticized.

to teachings which are authoritative but noninfallible; thus we prescind from the question of the possibility and the limits of licit dissent from such teachings. Fourth, we prescind from the question whether Vatican II in *Gaudium et spes* 51, with footnote 14, reaffirmed the received teaching or refrained from reaffirming it.[11]

We assume that the Catholic Church enjoys the charism of infallibility both in believing and in teaching and that this divine gift extends to the acts by which certain particular truths—including certain moral norms in respect to specific kinds of human acts—are believed and handed on. We also assume that the ordinary Magisterium of the bishops dispersed throughout the world is exercised infallibly under the conditions articulated by Vatican II in *Lumen gentium* 25.

We realize that some who reject the received Catholic teaching on the morality of contraception also reject what we assume with respect to the Church's infallibility.[12] However, we also are convinced that most

[11] While we prescind from the question of what Vatican II taught on the substantive issue, we will rely upon Vatican II's clear teaching regarding the competence of the Magisterium to teach with respect to the morality of contraception a norm binding on conscience. Furthermore, we set aside here the substantive issue only because it is unnecessary for our present purpose to treat it. We would, if necessary, defend all but minor details of the position stated by John C. Ford, S.J., "State of the Question: More on the Council and Contraception", *America* 114 (Apr. 16, 1966): 553–57.

[12] Only a few go to the extreme of rejecting infallibility in general, but some deny it to the extent that it guarantees the teaching of moral norms binding on conscience with respect to specific kinds of human acts; see, e.g., the authors cited by Richard A. McCormick, S.J., "Notes on Moral Theology: January–June, 1969", *TS* 30 (1969):

Catholics who accept what we assume in respect to infallibility and who, nevertheless, question or deny the received teaching on the morality of contraception have overlooked the possibility that this moral norm has been infallibly taught. Our argument is addressed to such Catholics, and we hope to show them that even if this teaching has not been defined, it has been infallibly taught by the ordinary Magisterium.

In section II we examine the conditions articulated by Vatican II under which the bishops dispersed throughout the world proclaim the teaching of Christ infallibly. In section III we argue that the facts show that the received Catholic teaching on the morality of contraception has been proposed infallibly by this ordinary Magisterium. In section IV we offer some further considerations and answer some objections. In section V we clarify the relationship between our present argument and the argument based upon tradition proposed by some theologians in the pontifical Commission for the Study of Problems of Population, Family, and Birthrate. In section VI we make some concluding remarks, with special reference to the statements of certain national hierarchies in response to *Humanae vitae*.

654–57. Others attempt to limit infallibility by adopting a relativistic theory of truth, especially of moral truth, according to which norms infallibly proposed until recently might suddenly have become false. The assumption we make in the present paper concerning the Church's infallibility is intended to exclude both the extreme position rejecting it altogether and such limited denials of it.

II

After treating the authoritative teaching office of the bishops and of the Pope, even when he is not speaking *ex cathedra*, Vatican II in *Lumen gentium* 25 proceeds to articulate the conditions under which the bishops dispersed throughout the world participate in the infallible proclamation of Christ's teaching:

> Although the bishops individually do not enjoy the prerogative of infallibility, they nevertheless proclaim the teaching of Christ infallibly, even when they are dispersed throughout the world, provided that they remain in communion with each other and with the successor of Peter and that in authoritatively teaching on a matter of faith and morals they agree in one judgment as that to be held definitively.[13]

Footnote 40, appended by the Council to this statement, refers to four previous documents.

To throw light upon this important text, we first follow its genesis in the proceedings of Vatican II. Second, we examine the texts to which footnote 40 refers.

[13] "Licet singuli praesules infallibilitatis praerogativa non polleant, quando tamen, etiam per orbem dispersi, sed communionis nexum inter se et cum Successore Petri servantes, authentice res fidei et morum docentes in unam sententiam tamquam definitive tenendam conveniunt, doctrinam Christi infallibiliter enunciant." The translation of this and other important texts we shall quote is our own; the sense of key expressions such as "to be held definitively" which will appear repeatedly in our discussion is intended to be the same as that of the corresponding Latin phrase, the meaning of which we will try to clarify.

Third, we discuss the conditions articulated for the infallible exercise of the ordinary Magisterium and how these conditions would be met, especially in the case of a teaching in a matter of morals.

The first schema of Vatican II on the Church was prepared before the Council opened. It was distributed at the first session, November 23, 1962; debate on it began December 1, 1962. Chapter 7 of this schema deals with the Magisterium of the Church. Article 29 states that the object of the authoritative Magisterium includes not only truths explicitly or implicitly revealed but also matters connected with the deposit of faith, necessary for integrally guarding it and rightly explicating it. Also, as minister of salvation, the Magisterium has the duty of interpreting and infallibly declaring not only the revealed law but also the natural law. Article 30 states that the primary holder of the authoritative teaching office is the Pope; by the very fact that he defines a doctrine, it is certain that it is contained in the revealed deposit or necessarily connected with it. The schema goes on to treat the teaching office of the bishops and seems to limit the infallibility of the ordinary Magisterium of the bishops dispersed throughout the world to cases in which they act as witnesses of faith in the handing on of *revealed doctrine*.[14]

---

[14] *Acta synodalia sacrosancti Concilii Oecumenici Vaticani II* 1/4 (Typis Polyglottis Vaticanis, 1971), 48–51, with commentary, p. 55, and notes pp. 57–59. A useful guide through the relevant documents of Vatican II is Umberto Betti, *La dottrina sull'episcopato nel capitolo III della costituzione dommatica Lumen gentium* (Roma: Città Nuova, 1968). His summary commentary (393–411) is very helpful for understand-

The sharply negative comments of the Council Fathers on this first schema on the Church hardly touched upon chapter 7. Constructive suggestions for a statement on the doctrinal authority of the college of bishops were made by Cardinal Feltin and the bishops of the province of Paris. They urged that the treatment begin with a quotation from Saint Irenaeus, stressing the unity of the teaching of the Church dispersed throughout the world. In the object of infallible teaching they wanted included points *necessarily conjoined* with revelation; the exercise of the supreme and infallible authority of the bishops they said to be either by solemn definition or by ordinary and universal Magisterium.[15]

The elaborate treatment of the Magisterium of the Church in the first schema of Vatican II not only treated the Magisterium of the Pope and of the bishops but also treated the participation of theologians, pastors, and the faithful at large in the Church's Magisterium. The second schema makes an altogether fresh start. The teaching office of the bishops is treated in article 19 in the context of a synthesis of teaching on the episcopacy, a synthesis the Council Fathers had demanded.

The bishops authoritatively preach and teach, drawing from the treasury of revelation new things and old, making the Faith fruitful, and defending their flocks

---

ing *Lumen gentium*, 25, and in what follows we rely upon his account for the development of the text between the sessions.

[15] *Acta synodalia* 1/4, 405–7.

against errors. The faithful must be responsive to such preaching and teaching. The schema goes on:

> Indeed, although the bishops individually do not enjoy the prerogative of infallibility, they nevertheless proclaim the teaching of Christ with an infallible utterance, even when they are dispersed throughout the world, provided that they remain in a collegial bond and that in authoritatively teaching as witnesses of faith in union with the Roman pontiff they agree in one judgment in handing on the revealed faith.[16]

This second schema adds that infallibility in defining extends as far as Christ willed that his Church enjoy this gift in defining. But then the schema seems to limit the scope of infallibility by saying that when the Pope or a council defines a proposition, they propose it to be *according to revelation itself.*[17]

This schema on the Church was prepared between the first and second sessions of Vatican II and was mailed to the Council Fathers during the spring or summer of 1963. Written comments were received and so an extensive list of proposed amendments to the

---

[16] *Acta synodalia sacrosancti Concilii Oecumenici Vaticani II* 2/1 (Typis Polyglottis Vaticanis, 1971), 238: "Imo, licet singuli praesules infallibilitatis praerogativa non polleant, quando tamen, etiam per orbem dispersi, sed collegialem nexum servantes, authentice docentes una cum Romano Pontifice ut testes fidei in revelata fide tradenda in unam sententiam conveniunt, doctrinam Christi infallibili oraculo enunciant." See also the notes, pp. 249–50.

[17] Ibid.: "Cum autem sive Romanus Pontifex sive Concilium sententiam definiunt, eam proferunt secundum ipsam Revelationem, cui omnes conformari tenentur. . . ."

first version of the second schema was available even before discussion on it began, September 30, 1963.

Bishop Fidelis García Martínez carefully developed an argument to show that the proposed formula would be overly restrictive with respect to the object of infallible teaching. Referring to the documents of Vatican I, he pointed out that a phrase in the proposed formula of papal infallibility, which would have limited it to cases in which the Pope defines a doctrine as to be held *of faith*, was amended in the final version to omit the restrictive words "of faith". García Martínez also pointed out that the Magisterium does not usually use the formula "to be held *of faith*" in proposing definitions. He argued that although Vatican I was broken off before it was able to complete its work, its documents make clear that the bishops agreed that infallibility is not limited to truths formally revealed but also extends to points that are implicitly or virtually revealed or necessarily connected with revelation. He urged that the statement of the object of infallible teaching be clarified by express language saying that it extends as far as the deposit of divine revelation *and the office of guarding and explicating it*, so that the Magisterium is infallible both in defining truths expressly contained in the deposit *and in defining truths necessarily connected with this deposit*, and in condemning opposed errors.[18]

Bishop Arturus Tabera Araoz also sought amendments to the schema to make clear that the object of

---

[18] Ibid., 317–18, with 664–68.

infallible teaching is not restricted to what is formally revealed.[19]

Bishop Francis Simons, on the contrary, wished to restrict the infallibility of the ordinary Magisterium to the really central and more important truths; other truths would be taught infallibly only if they were solemnly defined. He wished to leave room for the possibility of error, although not of really harmful error, in the teaching proposed by the ordinary and universal Magisterium.[20]

Discussion on the floor of the Council of the chapter on the episcopacy in the new schema focused upon collegiality and other topics. However, when debate on this chapter was cut off on October 16, 1963, written comments were invited. Some of these are relevant.

Cardinal Bea asked what was meant in the concrete by the "collegial bond" required in the formula, quoted above, of the infallibility of the bishops dispersed throughout the world. He also suggested that restricting infallible definition to matters proposed *according to revelation itself* would be restricting it too much, since not everything which belongs to the deposit of faith necessarily comes from revelation properly so called.[21] Bishop Charles G. Maloney also wanted to avoid restricting the object of infallibility.[22]

---

[19] Ibid., 736–37.
[20] Ibid., 317, with 727.
[21] *Acta synodalia sacrosancti Concilii Oecumenici Vaticani II* 2/2 (Typis Polyglottis Vaticanis, 1972), 650.
[22] Ibid., 803–4.

Bishop Antonius de Castro Mayer, on the contrary, objected that the teaching of the bishops dispersed throughout the world was not *strictly* a collegial act. From this he argued that their teaching as such would not be infallible, since the mere objective agreement of many fallible acts could not render them infallible. He wished the Council to say only that when the bishops agree *in handing on divine revelation*, the doctrine they propose must pertain to the revealed deposit, and for this reason such a doctrine should be believed by everyone.[23]

An amended text of the second schema on the Church was presented September 15, 1964, as the third session began. Several of the amendments made together with the official reasons given for making them deserve close attention for understanding the final text. Article 19 of the previous text became article 25 of the amended text, which is close to *Lumen gentium* 25, as we now have it.

"Collegial bond" is replaced with "bond of communion" to avoid the disputed question whether there is verified a *strictly* collegial act in the ordinary and universal Magisterium.[24] Thus the Council prescinds from the requirement of collegiality when it teaches that the

[23] Ibid., 721–23; these remarks were entered in the name of eight other bishops as well.

[24] *Acta synodalia sacrosancti Concilii Oecumenici Vaticani II* 3/1 (Typis Polyglottis Vaticanis, 1973), 250–51: "Loco 'sed collegialem nexum servantes' (T.P., p. 67, 1. 39 s.), ponitur '*communionis* nexum servantes', ad vitandam quaestionem disputatam utrum in magisterio ordinario et universali verificetur actus stricte collegialis, prouti in Concilio Oecumenico habetur."

bishops dispersed throughout the world proclaim the doctrine of Christ infallibly—and in so teaching Vatican II overrides the argument articulated by Bishop de Castro Mayer.

"In handing on the revealed faith" is replaced with "teaching on matters of faith and morals", to avoid restricting the infallibility of the episcopal body to those points which are proposed by it to be believed as divinely revealed. "As witnesses of faith" is also omitted, because this was already stressed enough. But a qualification is added: the infallibility of the bishops is in question only when they propose a judgment as one *to be held definitively*.[25] Thus the Council leaves the ambit of infallibility open to matters not divinely revealed and so meets the objections of Bishop Martínez and the reservations of Cardinal Bea[26] and Bishop Maloney—while conceding nothing to the demand of Bishop Simons for greater restrictiveness.

Both the prior text and the amended one proceed from their statement of the infallibility of the bishops

[25] Ibid., 251: "Pro verbis: 'in revelata fide tradenda' (T.P., pp. 67–68, 1. 41–1), ponuntur verba '*res fidei et morum* docentes', ne videatur infallibilitas corporis episcopalis coarctari tantum ad ea quae ab eodem ut divinitus revelata credenda proponuntur. Additur tamen quod agitur de casu quo proponunt sententiam *tamquam definitive tenendam*. Pariter, in eadem linea, omittuntur verba *ut testes fidei*, cum illa qualitas Episcoporum in eorum magisterio authentico sat superque includatur."

[26] The phrase to which Cardinal Bea took exception (see n. 17 above) remains in the final paragraph of *Lumen gentium*, 25, but the amendments make clear that "secundum" should not be understood in a restrictive sense; what is required to guard revelation as inviolable and expound it with fidelity also is "secundum ipsam Revelationem".

dispersed throughout the world to a statement on the more manifest case of infallible teaching: when the bishops in council define. The prior text says that such definitions ought to be accepted "with a sincere mind". The amended text substitutes "with the allegiance of faith", in order to distinguish the assent due to infallible teaching from that due to authoritative but noninfallible teaching. But since the allegiance of faith admits various degrees of adhesion, a generic formula, "allegiance of faith", rather than "allegiance of *divine* faith" is adopted.[27] Thus the Council carefully makes room for cases in which the assent with which an infallible teaching is held definitively is an act of faith, but not an act of divine faith—that is, cases in which a truth not divinely revealed is infallibly taught.

The prior text was not clear and complete with respect to the object of infallibility, since it simply said that it extends as far as Christ willed his Church to

---

[27] Ibid.: "Loco antiquioris formulae (T.P., p. 68, 1. 7): 'sincero animo accipi debent' haec ponitur, quo melius urgeatur adhaesio definitionibus Concilii debita. Quae talis est, ut *sinceram animi adhaesionem superet*, quippe quae, ubi de definitionibus agitur, obsequium fidei penitus attingat: quod quidem fidei obsequium gradus diversos admittit iuxta maiorem vel minorem relationem veritatis definitae cum divina Revelatione. Ad hunc disparem adhaesionis gradum, adhibetur formula generica '*fidei obsequio*', non autem: 'fidei *divinae* obsequio'." This explanation bears directly upon the assent due to a *conciliar definition*, but it nevertheless makes clear that the Council leaves room for a case in which a truth not formally revealed is infallibly taught, and if there is room for such a case when the bishops in council define, there obviously also is room for such a case when they exercise their ordinary Magisterium infallibly.

be infallible in defining doctrine concerning faith or morals. The amended text puts the statement of the extent of the object of infallibility in better order and completes it. This statement is located immediately after the statement of the infallibility of the bishops whether dispersed throughout the world or gathered in council: "Now this infallibility, with which the divine Redeemer willed his Church to be endowed in defining doctrine of faith or morals, extends as far as extends the deposit of divine revelation, which must be guarded as inviolable and expounded with fidelity."[28] The explanation of this amendment makes two important points. The infallibility with which Christ wished his Church to be endowed is identified with the infallibility of the teaching Church. The object of the infallibility of the Church has the same extent as the revealed deposit, and so it extends to all things and only to things "which either directly belong to the revealed deposit itself, or which are required to guard as inviolable and expound with fidelity this same deposit".[29]

[28] Ibid., 221: "Haec autem infallibilitas, qua Divinus Redemptor Ecclesiam suam in definienda doctrina de fide vel moribus instructam esse voluit, tantum patet quantum divinae Revelationis patet depositum, sancte custodiendum et fideliter exponendum." The relationship between the last clause and the one which precedes it is almost impossible to capture in English, but the official explanation makes clear that what is meant is: the deposit of divine revelation *and* what is required to guard it as inviolable and expound it with fidelity.

[29] Ibid., 251: "Verba 'In definitionibus suis . . . esse voluit' (T.P., lin. 8–11) aliter ordinantur et notabiliter *complentur*, ut haec duo

Having received this amended text together with the explanations we have been discussing, the Fathers of Vatican II cast many separate votes on chapter 3 of the amended text. The text of the paragraph on the infallible teaching office of the bishops, whether dispersed throughout the world or united in council, was the subject of their twenty-fifth ballot; the single sentence quoted above, regarding the extent of infallibility, was the subject of their twenty-sixth ballot. The former was approved by a vote of 2,134 to 63 with 1 null ballot; the latter was approved by a vote of 2,159 to 32 with 1 null ballot.[30]

In these votes amendments were proposed. However, none of them was accepted; the text voted upon is that of *Lumen gentium*. Nevertheless, the disposition of two of the proposed amendments is of interest. One of them, although proposed for a different reason—to avoid any implication that a strictly collegial act was required for the infallible teaching of the bishops dispersed throughout the world—would have restored "to be held of faith" in place of the amended text's "to

---

indubitanter affirmentur: *a*) Infallibilitas qua Christus Ecclesiam instructam esse voluit prorsus *identificatur* cum infallibilitate Ecclesiae docentis; et quidem: sive totius Episcopatus, sive singulariter Romani Pontificis. *b*) *Obiectum infallibilitatis* Ecclesiae, ita explicatae, eamdem habet extensionem ac depositum revelatum; ideoque extenditur ad ea omnia, et ad ea tantum, quae vel directe ad ipsum depositum revelatum spectant, vel quae ad idem depositum sancte custodiendum et fideliter exponendum requiruntur, ut habetur in Conc. Vat. I: Denz. 1836 (3070), ubi de infallibilitate Romani Pontificis."

[30] Ibid., 406; *Acta synodalia sacrosancti Concilii Oecumenici Vaticani II* 3/8 (Typis Polyglottis Vaticanis, 1976), 53.

be held definitively". This amendment was rejected with the explanation that the approved text in no way suggests that the teaching act in question is strictly collegial.[31]

Another proposed amendment sought a statement concerning the infallibility of the Church in matters *connected* with the deposit of divine revelation. This demand was rejected with the explanation that what was sought is stated equivalently in the lines which state that infallibility "extends as far as the deposit of divine revelation, which must be guarded as inviolable and expounded with fidelity".[32] This response confirmed the previous interpretation of the language adopted, which admits within the scope of infallibility points which do not directly belong to the revealed deposit but which are necessary to guard and expound this deposit.

Our examination of the development of the text of *Lumen gentium* 25 makes two things clear. First, Vatican II purposely avoided saying that a strictly collegial act is required for the infallibility of the ordinary Magisterium of the bishops. Second, the Council also studiously avoided limiting the infallibility of such teaching to cases in which a point divinely revealed is proposed for acceptance with the assent of divine faith.

We now proceed to consider four previous documents to which Vatican II refers in its footnote 40, appended to *Lumen gentium* 25, regarding the infallibility with which the bishops dispersed throughout the world proclaim the doctrine of Christ. The note first

[31] Ibid., 89.   [32] Ibid.

refers to Vatican I, *Dei Filius*, chapter 3: "Further, all those things are to be believed with divine and Catholic faith which are contained in the word of God, written or handed down, and which the Church either by a solemn judgment or by her ordinary and universal Magisterium proposes for belief as divinely revealed."[33] Since *Dei Filius* is concerned with divine revelation, this solemn teaching is limited to what is proposed as revealed and to be believed with divine faith. However, it is relevant to the teaching of Vatican II insofar as it definitively teaches that the scope of what must be believed is not restricted to what is defined but extends to points proposed by the universal and ordinary Magisterium.

The note of Vatican II goes on to refer to a passage added to Vatican I's first schema *De ecclesia*; this passage, as Vatican II notes, is drawn from Bellarmine, who in rejecting Protestant qualifications of the Church's infallibility writes:

> Therefore, our view is that the Church *absolutely* cannot err, either in things absolutely necessary [for salvation] or in other matters which she proposes to us to be believed or to be done, whether expressly included in the Scriptures or not. And when we say "The Church cannot err", we understand this to apply both to the faithful as a whole and to the bishops as a whole, so that the

---

[33] DS (ed. 34) 1792 (3011): "Porro fide divina et catholica ea omnia credenda sunt, quae in verbo Dei scripto vel tradito continentur et ab Ecclesia sive solemni iudicio sive ordinario et universali magisterio tamquam divinitus revelata credenda proponuntur." In Vatican II's official note, a typographical error makes the reference read: "1712 (3011)".

sense of the proposition *The Church cannot err* is this: that what all the faithful hold as of faith, necessarily is true and of faith, and similarly what all the bishops teach as pertaining to faith, necessarily is true and of faith.[34]

Bellarmine's statement refers explicitly not only to things which are to be *believed* but also to things which are to be *done*. He also excludes limiting the scope of infallibility to matters treated explicitly in Scripture or to matters which are absolutely essential for salvation.

The quotation from Bellarmine, although drawn from a schema of Vatican I which was never completed, attains a status which it would not have of itself, because it is cited by Vatican II as expressing a teaching comparable with its own. The same is true of the third document to which Vatican II refers in its note, Vatican I's revised schema of Constitution 2, *De ecclesia Christi*, together with Kleutgen's commentary:

> And so we now define that this very high gift, by which *the Church of the living God is the pillar and bulwark*

[34] J. D. Mansi et al., *Sacrorum conciliorum nova et amplissima collectio* 51 (Arnhem & Leipzig: H. Welter, 1926), 579C: "Nostra igitur sententia est, ecclesiam *absolute* non posse errare, nec in rebus absolute necessariis, nec in aliis quae credenda vel facienda nobis proponit, sive habeantur expresse in Scripturis sive non. Et cum dicimus, ecclesiam non posse errare, id intelligimus tam de universitate fidelium quam de universitate episcoporum, ita ut sensus sit eius propositionis, *ecclesia non potest errare*, id est, id quod tenent omnes fideles tanquam de fide, necessario est verum et de fide, et similiter id, quod docent omnes episcopi tanquam ad fidem pertinens, necessario est verum et de fide." Italics in Mansi.

of truth [1 Tim 3:15], is placed in it so that neither the faithful as a whole in believing nor those who are appointed with the power of teaching the whole Church in exercising this office can fall into error. Therefore, all those points which in matters of faith and morals are everywhere held or handed down as undoubted under bishops in communion with the Apostolic See, as well as all those points which are defined, either by those same bishops together with the Roman pontiff or by the Roman pontiff speaking *ex cathedra*, are to be held as infallibly true.[35]

This formulation of the Church's infallibility, including the infallibility of the bishops dispersed throughout the world, is very close to that finally adopted by Vatican II, especially in avoiding the limitation of infallibility to points divinely revealed and proposed for acceptance with an assent of divine faith. The parallel to Vatican II's "to be held *definitively*" in Vatican I's schema is "held or handed down as *undoubted*".

This mode of expression supports the position that truths required to preserve and unfold the deposit of

---

[35] Mansi 53, 313AB: "Iam vero praecelsum hoc donum, quo *ecclesia Dei vivi columna et firmamentum veritatis est* [reference to 1 Tim 3:15], in eo positum esse definimus, ut n que fideles universi credendo, nec ii, qui potestate docendi totam ecclesiam praediti sunt, cum hoc munere funguntur, in errorem labi possint. Quaecumque igitur in rebus fidei et morum ubique locorum sub episcopis apostolicae sedi adhaerentibus tanquam indubitata tenentur vel traduntur, necnon quae sive ab iisdem episcopis, accedente Romani pontificis confirmatione, sive ab ipso Romano pontifice ex cathedra loquente ab omnibus tenenda et tradenda definiuntur, ea pro infallibiliter veris habenda sunt."

faith can be taught infallibly by the ordinary Magisterium even if they are not divinely revealed. The commentary of Kleutgen expands at length on this point, enlarging rather than delimiting the scope of the ordinary Magisterium and making a case for the position that the Church can teach infallibly on moral questions with respect to which revelation says nothing either explicitly or implicitly.[36]

The final document to which Vatican II refers in footnote 40 is Pius IX's letter *Tuas libenter*.[37] Pope Pius especially stresses in the passage cited that the submission of the act of divine faith cannot be limited to defined dogmas; this is the position which Vatican I subsequently incorporated in *Dei Filius*. The only interesting point which the papal letter makes that is not

[36] Mansi 53, 324–31. The final text of Vatican II's footnote does not provide page numbers in the reference to Kleutgen's commentary; the first text of the second schema misidentifies the proposed conciliar *text* as pertaining to the commentary, and then refers to a very brief statement at the beginning of the commentary proper (*Acta synodalia* 2/1, 249–50). On this basis, it does not seem that Vatican II's final reference ought to be read as an endorsement of Kleutgen's entire commentary, yet the commentary remains a very authoritative guide to what the proposed text of Vatican I meant. Moreover, it cannot be ruled out altogether that the note of Vatican II does refer to the entire commentary; all of it is relevant to the passage of the schema which is specifically cited. In recent years, it has often been said that Bishop Gasser, the *relator* of Vatican I's chapter on papal infallibility in *Pastor aeternus*, limited the extent of infallibility to *formally revealed* truths. But his explanation (Mansi 52, 1221–27 and 1316–17) clearly says that there is a secondary object of infallible teaching; Gasser held the affirmation of such a secondary object to be theologically certain, though not *de fide*.

[37] DS 1683 (2879).

touched upon in the other documents is that the universal and constant consensus of Catholic theologians holding a point as pertaining to faith is evidence that the matter is one handed on by the ordinary Magisterium of the Church dispersed throughout the world.

We are now in a position to comment upon the conditions, articulated by Vatican II, under which the bishops, dispersed throughout the world, proclaim the doctrine of Christ infallibly. There are four conditions: first, that the bishops remain in communion with one another and with the Pope; second, that they teach authoritatively on a matter of faith or morals; third, that they agree in one judgment; and fourth, that they propose this judgment as one to be held definitively.

The first condition, as the evolution of the text shows, does not demand that the bishops act in a strictly collegial manner. No single act making explicit the intent to teach together is required. As Irenaeus says in the passage quoted by Cardinal Feltin: "The Church, although scattered throughout the whole world, diligently guards [the Faith] as if she lived in one house; and similarly she believes these [truths], just as if she had one mind and one heart, and she harmoniously preaches and teaches and hands on these [truths], as if she possessed one mouth."[38] The bond of communion by which bishops remain in the Catholic Church—a bond broken by separated brethren—is necessary and sufficient for the bishops to share in the Church's united guarding, preaching, teaching, and handing on of the

[38] *Against Heresies*, 1, 10, 2 (PG 7, 552).

Faith. By the same token, dissident judgments by bishops who do not maintain the bond of communion do not detract from the unity of judgment which is also required—the third of the conditions listed above—for the bishops to teach infallibly.

The second condition, that the bishops teach authoritatively on a matter of faith or morals, makes explicit the requirement that the bishops be teaching in their official capacity, not merely expressing views as personal opinions or in their capacity as private theologians. The expression "faith and morals" used to refer to the subject matter in which the Magisterium is competent is a formula with a long history.[39] But nothing in the documentation we have examined warrants restricting the scope of "morals" as used by Vatican II to exclude specific moral norms, such as that on contraception. Moreover, Vatican II itself, in *Gaudium et spes* 51, at least affirmed the competency of the Magisterium in this very matter when it stated: "Relying on these principles, it is not allowed that children of the Church in regulating procreation should use methods which are disapproved of by the Magisterium in its explaining of the divine law."[40] The recognition of the proposal of a *moral* teaching as one to be held definitively has certain special features which we shall discuss at the end of the present section.

---

[39] See M. Bévenot, "Faith and Morals in Vatican I and in the Council of Trent", *Heythrop Journal* 3 (1962): 15–30.

[40] *Gaudium et spes*, 51: "Filiis Ecclesiae, his principiis innixis, in procreatione regulanda, vias inire non licet, quae a Magisterio, in lege divina explicanda, improbantur."

The third condition for infallibility in the teaching of the bishops dispersed throughout the world is that they agree in one judgment. The ordinary Magisterium must be *universal* if it is to be infallible; this is explicit in the solemn teaching of Vatican I in *Dei Filius* as well as in Pius IX's letter *Tuas libenter*. According to the note of Bellarmine and the second schema *De ecclesia Christi* of Vatican I, the infallibility of the Church is present in the believing of the faithful *as a whole* and in the teaching of the bishops united with the Pope *as a whole*.

The first thing to note about this required universality is that it is the moral unity of the whole body of bishops in communion with each other and with the Pope, not the mathematical unanimity of the bishops which would be broken by the dissenting voice of any one individual. This point is made abundantly clear by an example used by Bishop Martin of Paderborn, when he explained in a speech at Vatican I what the Deputation of Faith intended in the paragraph—cited by Vatican II and quoted above—in which it formulated the point that the ordinary and universal Magisterium determines an object of faith when it proposes something to be believed even without defining it. Martin's example was this: All Catholic bishops believed in the divinity of Christ before the Council of Nicaea, but this doctrine was not openly defined and openly declared until that Council; therefore, in the time before the Council of Nicaea, this dogma was taught by the ordinary Magisterium.[41] As everyone knows, there was

---

[41] Mansi 51, 224–25.

mathematical unanimity among Catholic bishops on this doctrine neither before the definition of Nicaea nor even after it, except insofar as those who dissented from the definitive teaching of Nicaea may have ceased to be Catholic bishops.

Another point about the required universality is that if this condition has been met for some period in the past, it is not nullified by lack of present consensus among Catholic bishops. Each future bishop until the end of time will in his day share in the Magisterium; the consensus of future bishops is not required for the Church to teach infallibly today. Just so, the present consensus of Catholic bishops was not required for the Church to teach infallibly in times past. A judgment once proposed by a body of teachers who could not err in proposing it and accepted by a body of believers who could not err in accepting it cannot subsequently be thrown into doubt because it is questioned or denied by some of the members of that body of teachers and believers; for each of these teachers can become a false prophet and each of these believers can be misled. What is once infallibly proposed must always afterward be accepted with absolute assurance of its truth. Once the truth about what Christ commanded has been proclaimed infallibly, every opinion incompatible with it must always afterward be excluded from gaining true normative force for the faith and life of the Church with which Christ remains forever.

It is only because the normative force of the teaching acts of present members of the Magisterium is conditioned by the consensus of the past that Christian teachers who have found themselves in disagreement about what is essential to Christian faith and life have always appealed to Tradition—that is, to what all *received* in common because all *were taught* the same things by a universal Magisterium previously of one mind, a single mind formed by the saving truths and moral norms of Christ's teaching, all of which spring from the one font of his gospel.[42] In appealing to Tradition, Christian teachers always have assumed that what is universally received cannot be contradicted and abandoned, although it can be unfolded and explained in new ways.

What sort of evidence of the required universality can we expect and should we demand? The evidence must be this: that a certain point of teaching has been proposed by bishops repeatedly, in different times, in different places, in response to different challenges; that the bishops have articulated and defended this point of teaching in different intellectual frameworks, perhaps reinforcing it with varying disciplinary measures. Moreover, there must be no evidence that the point of teaching has ever been questioned or denied by any bishop or by anyone else authorized to participate in the Church's teaching mission without eliciting an admonition and a reaffirmation of what had been universally taught. Obviously, one cannot expect or demand positive evidence that every bishop has proposed the same teaching; available historical sources always will fall short of establishing so extensive a set of factual

[42] Vatican II, *Dei verbum*, 7; cf. Council of Trent, DS 783 (1501).

conclusions. To demand such evidence would be to set up an arbitrary barrier against every appeal to Tradition.

In considering the evidence for the universality of a particular teaching in times past, the statements of Christians who were not bishops can be regarded as providing some evidence for universality. As Pius IX made clear, members of the Church who are not members of the hierarchical Magisterium can participate in and bear witness to the infallible teaching of the ordinary Magisterium. For example, theologians authorized by the bishops to teach and teaching in harmony with them share in their role.

Further, corresponding to the infallibility of the ordinary Magisterium in teaching is the infallibility of the whole body of the faithful in believing.[43] Indeed, infallibility in teaching and infallibility in believing—like giving a gift and receiving the same gift—are two aspects of one reality, considered from relationally opposite points of view. Consequently, even the "last of the faithful" who receives the word of God and keeps it can contribute to the handing on of Christian faith and morals through his words, his religious and devotional acts, and his living a life suitable to one called with a vocation such as his.[44] Hence, evidence of the faith and practice of Christians generally, to the extent that their beliefs and lives were in harmony with what

---

[43] A point which was expressly stated by Bellarmine (see n. 34 above) and included in Vatican I's schema *De ecclesia* (see n. 35 above) and taught by Vatican II, *Lumen gentium*, 12.

[44] Cf. *Lumen gentium*, 35; *Apostolicam actuositatem*, 6.

we know of the teaching of the ordinary Magisterium, can supply evidence in support of the universality of the teaching of that Magisterium.

The fourth condition for infallibility in the exercise of the ordinary Magisterium is that the bishops agree in proposing one judgment to be held *definitively*. "To be held definitively" does not seem to be an expression with a previous theological history.[45] It cannot mean that the infallible teaching of the ordinary Magisterium must be expressed in the language of solemn definition. The bishops dispersed throughout the world do not define and do not use the language of solemn definition, except when they quote some solemn definition previously made by the Church.

The genesis of the text makes clear that what is demanded if the exercise of the ordinary Magisterium is to be infallible is that a judgment be proposed for acceptance with an assent of certitude, similar to the assent of divine faith but not necessarily having the

[45] The important distinction between "to be believed" and "to be held" was made by Vatican I in defining papal infallibility; see J. Salaverri, S.J., *De ecclesia Christi* 3, nos. 909–10, in M. Nicolau, S.J., and J. Salaverri, S.J., *Sacrae theologiae summa*, vol. 1, *Theologia fundamentalis* (Madrid: B.A.C., 1962), 801–3. "Definitive" was not necessary in *Pastor aeternus*, because Vatican I is concerned there precisely with *definitions*. "Definitive" has irrelevant technical uses in medieval authors such as Saint Thomas. However, in a submission by the Universitas Catholica "Sophia" to the prepreparatory commission for Vatican II, "tamquam definitive ab omnibus fidelibus tenenda tradantur" does appear in a proposal that the forthcoming Council teach that the ordinary Magisterium can be exercised infallibly: *Acta et documenta Concilio Oecumenico Vaticano II apparando*, ser. 1, vol. 4, pars 2 (Typis Polyglottis Vaticanis, 1961), 567.

same motive as has the latter assent. The formula in the second schema *De ecclesia Christi* of Vatican I, which Vatican II cites as comparable with its own teaching, refers to points held or handed down *as undoubted*. Thus, "to be held definitively" clearly excludes cases in which a bishop proposes a view as a safe and probable opinion but only as such.

A point of teaching surely is proposed as one to be held definitively if a bishop proposes it in the following way: not at his option but as part of his duty to hand on the teaching he has received; not as doubtful or even as very probable but as certainly true; and not as one which the faithful are free to accept or to reject but as one which every Catholic must accept.

When teachings on matters of morality are proposed, it would be a mistake to give an exclusively intellectualist sense to the expression "to be held definitively". The Church often proposes what Christians must do to be saved by exhortation and preaching, which calls more directly for action than for intellectual assent. Intellectual assent is required, of course. But moral precepts demand something more: a sincere effort, at least, to fulfill the demand. Thus one who proposes a moral teaching as a point to be held definitively is not likely to say explicitly that this point deserves assent as a truth. Rather, he is likely to say that the teaching should be received as the will of God, which followers of Christ will try to live up to.

At the same time, one must distinguish the teaching of moral truths from the making of ecclesiastical laws, which are necessary for the good order of the Church.

The distinction is not always easy to keep in view, since the same language often is used in carrying out the two quite different functions of the bishops. However, moral teachings are characterized by the fact that they are proposed as norms which are received by the Magisterium and which cannot be altered by ecclesiastical authority. The expressions "divine law" and "natural law" and "divine and natural law" often are used in recent documents of the Magisterium in reference to moral teachings. Such expressions are never used to refer to ecclesiastical laws; these latter are proposed as practical dictates which are laid down and which can be changed as necessary by the governing authority of the Pope and/or the bishops.

The teaching of Vatican II concerning the infallibility of the universal and ordinary Magisterium is not in substance new. Christians always have believed that the apostles and their successors in proclaiming the doctrine of Christ, although dispersed throughout the world and the centuries, enjoy an unfailing charism of truth. Saint Vincent of Lérins already attempted to formulate the conditions for the infallible exercise of the ordinary Magisterium, and he insisted at the same time upon the possibility of genuine development of doctrine.[46] Vatican II's more precise articulation of the conditions under which the ordinary Magisterium is exercised infallibly seems to us to have a providential timeliness.

In recent years those questioning received Catholic

---

[46] *Commonitorium primum*, 2 and 23 (PL 50, 639–40 and 667–69).

teachings frequently have adopted a method of dividing the sources from which the Church has her assurance of the truth of these teachings. Can the point of teaching be established with certitude from Sacred Scripture? If not, can the point of teaching be established with certitude to have its historical origin in apostolic preaching? If not, can the point of teaching be established with certitude by an authoritative but admittedly nondefinitive pronouncement of the contemporary Magisterium? If not, can the point of teaching be established with certitude by rational arguments to the satisfaction of philosophers who do not even agree upon the proper method of philosophical argumentation? If the point of teaching can be established in none of these ways, surely it is open to question and perhaps false. The received teaching must be rethought; a substitute more acceptable to men and women of today must be admitted.

The universal and ordinary Magisterium reintegrates what this method divides. The ordinary Magisterium guards and expounds the deposit of divine revelation and guides the faithful in reading Scripture so that they hear in it the saving word of God. The ordinary Magisterium is the living voice of Tradition, universally repeating as if with one mouth the common patrimony of faith. The universal and ordinary Magisterium of the past provides the sure foundation upon which the Pope and the bishops today can confidently proclaim the constant and very firm teaching of the Church. And the consensus of Catholic bishops in one judgment enlightens the mind even in those matters to which its power naturally extends, so that the sophistries which are at odds with faith are exposed and the Christian philosophies which promote understanding of saving truth are confirmed and commended.

III

In this section we show that the received Catholic teaching on the morality of contraception meets the conditions set down by Vatican II and thus is an infallible teaching. We first show that the received teaching was *universally proposed by Catholic bishops* up to 1962. Then we show that this *moral norm was authoritatively proposed as one to be held definitively*. Finally, we look at the great papal statements of Pius XI, Pius XII, and Paul VI in the light of the Church's previous teaching and belief.

Although the historical study of contraception by John T. Noonan, Jr., is defective in certain respects, it does offer substantial evidence for the universality of the Catholic Church's teaching on contraception up to 1962. This evidence is summed up by Noonan himself:

> The propositions constituting a condemnation of contraception are, it will be seen, recurrent. Since the first clear mention of contraception by a Christian theologian, when a harsh third-century moralist accused a pope of encouraging it, the articulated judgment has been the same. In the world of the late Empire known to St. Jerome and St. Augustine, in the Ostrogothic Arles of Bishop Caesarius and the Suevian Braga of Bishop Martin, in the Paris of St. Albert and St.

Thomas, in the Renaissance Rome of Sixtus V and the Renaissance Milan of St. Charles Borromeo, in the Naples of St. Alphonsus Liguori and the Liège of Charles Billuart, in the Philadelphia of Bishop Kenrick, and in the Bombay of Cardinal Gracias, the teachers of the Church have taught without hesitation or variation that certain acts preventing procreation are gravely sinful. No Catholic theologian has ever taught, "Contraception is a good act." The teaching on contraception is clear and apparently fixed forever.[47]

Noonan's book was published in 1965. Since that time a great number of theologians and other scholars, including many who think that contraception could be accepted as moral by the Church, have interested themselves in the subject. Collectively these scholars certainly have a very thorough acquaintance with the data; they surely would have published any evidence that the universality of the Church's teaching was interrupted by the contrary teaching of any bishop or of any other competent spokesman of Catholic thought. But no such evidence has come to light, and so there is a compelling reason to think that no such evidence exists.

We conclude that the historical evidence shows that Catholic bishops dispersed throughout the world

---

[47] John T. Noonan, Jr., *Contraception: A History of Its Treatment by the Catholic Theologians and Canonists* (Cambridge, Mass.: Harvard University, 1965), 6. Noonan immediately proceeds to call the apparent fixity into question and suggests that there might be room for a development of doctrine which would contradict the received teaching. We consider this suggestion in section IV.

agreed in one judgment on the morality of contraception, a judgment which remained substantially the same and which was universally proposed at least until 1962. The weight of this uniform teaching can be gauged more accurately if one considers certain facts, most of which are recorded by Noonan in his work.

First, not only Jerome and Augustine but also certain Eastern Fathers such as Epiphanius and Chrysostom condemned contraception.[48] Second, many of those who taught that acts intended to prevent procreation are gravely evil were bishops; many who were not bishops are canonized saints, including several who were Doctors of the Church. Third, the canon law of the universal Church from the thirteenth century until 1917 included the canon *Si aliquis*: "If anyone for the sake of fulfilling sexual desire or with premeditated hatred does something to a man or to a woman, or gives something to drink, so that he cannot generate, or she cannot conceive, or offspring be born, let it be held as homicide."[49] Of course, the old canon law included many disciplinary rules which were subject to change and were recognized to be such.

[48] Ibid., 96–99; Ambrose also is mentioned (99) as perhaps condemning contraception.

[49] *Corpus iuris canonici*, ed. A. L. Richter and A. Friedberg (Leipzig: Tauchnitz, 1881), 2, 794: "Si aliquis causa explendae libidinis vel odii meditatione homini aut mulieri aliquid fecerit, vel ad potandum dederit, ut non possit generare, aut concipere, vel nasci soboles, ut homicida teneatur." Noonan (178) translates "causa explendae libidinis", which is broad enough to cover all motivation by sexual impulse, "to satisfy his lust", which unnecessarily limits the motive to habitual vice.

But this canon was placed in a book on crimes, and nothing was classed as a crime unless it was considered to be a grave sin. It might be objected that this canon was null, since there is little if any historical evidence that persons who practiced contraception were treated as murderers. But this objection overlooks the teaching function of canon law, which functioned in moral formation analogously to the way in which creeds function in the handing on of the essentials of doctrine: As creeds summarize saving truth, canon law from the Middle Ages until 1917 codified moral formation. The *Roman Catechism* of 1566, authorized by the Council of Trent and prepared under Saint Pius V, incorporated the teaching of *Si aliquis* as to the use of medicines to impede procreation.[50]

Fourth, there is a constant consensus of Catholic theologians in modern times. This consensus is important because any indefiniteness in the Tradition regarding methods of contraception, its sinfulness in every single act, and other matters was eliminated either by the explicit statements of the modern theologians or by the general principles which they shared in common. This is especially true of the works in moral theology generally in use in the nineteenth and twentieth centuries.[51]

---

[50] Noonan, *Contraception*, 361.

[51] This point can be verified by an examination of some of the most used manuals (we include a few in canon law and pastoral medicine): (1) J. Aertnys, C.Ss.R., and C. A. Damen, C.Ss.R., *Theologia moralis* 2, 17th ed. (Turin: Marietti, 1956–58), nos. 893–95; (2) G. d'Annibale (Cardinal), *Summula theologiae moralis* 2, 5th ed. (Rome: Desclée,

We are not saying that all of the principles shared by moral theologians during this period deserve the same respect as the Church's substantive moral teaching. We are only saying that their shared principles

---

1908), n. 65; 3, n. 469; (3) J. Antonelli, *Medicina pastoralis in usum confessariorum* 2, 5th ed. (Rome: Pustet, 1932), 192–93; (4) A. M. Arregui, S.J., *Summarium theologiae moralis*, 20th ed. (Bilbao: Mesajero del Corazón de Jesús, 1952), nos. 813–14; (5) A. Ballerini, S.J., *Opus theologicum morale in Busenbaum Medullam*, ed. D. Palmieri, S.J., 6 (Prati: Giachetti, 1889–93), nos. 439–51; (6) J. de Becker, *De matrimonio*, 9th ed. (Louvain: Ceuterick, 1931), 125; (7) A. Berardi, *Praxis confessariorum seu moralis theologia theorico-practica* 1, 3d ed. (Faenza: Novelli, 1898–99), nos. 957–61; (8) G. Bucceroni, S.J., *Institutiones theologiae moralis* 4, 6th ed. (Rome: Pont. Inst. Pii IX, 1914–15), no. 1067; (9) C. F. N. Capellmann, *Pastoralmedizin*, ed. W. Bergmann, 17th ed. (Paderborn: Bonifacius, 1914), 260; (10) F. M. Cappello, S.J., *Tractatus canonico-moralis de sacramentis* 5, 7th ed. (Turin: Marietti, 1911), no. 816; (11) H. Davis, S.J., *Moral and Pastoral Theology*, ed. L. W. Geddes, S.J., 4, 7th ed. (London: Sheed & Ward, 1958), 260–61; (12) J. Ferreres, S.J., *Compendium theologiae moralis*, ed. A. Mondria, S.J., 2, 17th ed. (Barcelona: Subirana, 1949–50), nos. 1078–79; (13) E. Génicot, S.J., and J. Salsmans, S.J., *Institutiones theologiae moralis*, ed. A. Gortebecke, S.J., 2, 17th ed. (Brussels: L'Ed. Universelle, 1951), no. 665; (14) T. M. J. Gousset (Cardinal), *Théologie morale à l'usage des curés et des confesseurs* 2, 5th ed. (Paris: Lecoffre, 1848), nos. 892–93; (15) J. P. Gury, S.J., *Compendium theologiae moralis*, ed. A. Ballerini, S.J., 2, 12th ed. (Prati: Giachetti, 1894), nos. 730, 733–34; (16) A. Haine, *Theologiae moralis elementa* 4 (Louvain: Fonteyn, 1882–84), 206; (17) F. Hürth, S.J., *De statibus* (Rome: Gregorian University, 1946), no. 702; (18) T. A. Iorio, S.J., *Theologia moralis* 3, 3d ed. (Naples: d'Auria, 1947), nos. 1202–6; (19) H. Jone, O.F.M.Cap., *Moral Theology* (Westminster, Md.: Newman, 1945), nos. 757–59; (20) F. P. Kenrick (Bishop), *Theologia moralis* 2 (Mechlin: Dessain, 1861) 300; (21) A. Koch, *A Handbook of Moral Theology*, ed. A. Preuss, 5 (St. Louis: Herder, 1918–24), 473; (22) A. Konings,

preclude suggestions that they did not all mean the same thing when they agreed, for example, that acts intended to impede procreation are intrinsically and gravely evil.

C.Ss.R., *Theologia moralis s. Alphonsi in compendium redacta* 1, 7th ed. (New York: Benziger, 1888), nos. 1649–53; (23) A. Lanza and P. Palazzini, *Theologia moralis: Appendix de castitate et luxuria* (Turin: Marietti, 1953), 107–12; (24) A. Lehmkuhl, S.J., *Theologia moralis* 2, 12th ed. (Freiburg: Herder, 1914), 1093–96; (25) S. A. Loiano, O.F.M.Cap., *Institutiones theologiae moralis* 5 (Turin: Marietti, 1950–52), nos. 156–59; (26) C. Marc, C.Ss.R., and X. Gestermann, C.Ss.R., *Institutiones morales alphonsianae* 2, 20th ed. (Lyons: Lutetiae, 1946), nos. 2114–15; (27) J. A. McHugh, O.P., and C. J. Callan, O.P., *Moral Theology: A Complete Course* 2 (New York: Wagner, 1958), no. 2620; (28) B. H. Merkelbach, O.P., *Summa theologiae moralis* 3, 8th ed. (Bruges: Desclée, 1949), nos. 954–55; (29) E. M. Müller (Bishop), *Theologia moralis*, ed. A. Schmukenschlaeger, 2, 8th ed. (Vienna: Mayer, 1899), 525–26; (30) A. Niedermeyer, *Handbuch der speziellen Pastoralmedizin* 1 (Vienna: Herder, 1949), 272–320; (31) H. Noldin, S.J., *Summa theologiae moralis*, ed. A. Schmitt, S.J., and G. Heinzel, S.J., 35th ed. (Innsbruck: F. Rauch, 1956), *Complementum de castitate*, nos. 72–73; (32) G. B. Pighi, *Cursus theologiae moralis* 4, 3d ed. (Verona: Cinquetti, 1921), nos. 608–9; (33) A. Piscetta, S.S., and A. Gennaro, S.S., *Elementa theologiae moralis* 7, 2d ed. (Turin: Internazionale, 1934), nos. 233–35; (34) D. M. Prümmer, O.P., *Manuale theologiae moralis*, ed. E. M. Münch, O.P., 3, 10th ed. (Barielem: Herder, 1945–46), nos. 699–700; (35) A. Sabetti, S.J., *Compendium theologiae moralis*, ed. T. Barrett, S.J., 31st ed. of Gury (New York: Pustet, 1926), nos. 937–41; (36) T. Slater, S.J., *A Manual of Moral Theology* 2, 5th ed. (New York: Benziger, 1925), 249; (37) A. de Smet, *De sponsalibus et matrimonio*, 4th ed. (Bruges: Beyaert, 1927), nos. 239–40; (38) A. Tanquerey, *Synopsis theologiae moralis et pastoralis*, ed. J. B. Bird and F. Cimetier, 1, 14th ed. (Paris: Desclée, 1955), supp., nos. 38–42; (39) A. Vermeersch, S.J., *Theologia moralis* 4, 3d ed. (Rome: Gregorian University, 1933–37), no. 76; (40) G. J.

The consensus of modern theologians supports the thesis that the received teaching was universally proposed by Catholic bishops, because the works of the theologians were authorized by the bishops for use in seminaries, and thus for the training of confessors who communicated Catholic moral teaching to the faithful in the confessional, in premarital instructions, in the preaching of missions, and so on. As authorized agents of the bishops—during centuries in which the bishops were careful not to share their teaching authority with theologians whose views they did not accept—these *approved authors* teaching in their manuals exercised in a real though mediate way the teaching authority of each and every bishop who sent his seminarians to seminaries in which these manuals were required textbooks.

Fifth, both the Holy See and many individual bishops and groups of bishops in the nineteenth and twentieth centuries insisted upon the received Catholic teaching. Of these acts Noonan says:

> The instructions from Rome from 1816 to 1930 had interacted with the acts of the national hierarchies. It would be a mistake, I believe, to see the national statements against contraception as dictated from Rome, or the Roman interventions as brought about by national demands. A common tradition and theological training,

---

Waffelaert (Bishop), *Tractatus theologici de virtutibus cardinalibus* 1 (Bruges: Vandenberghe-Denaux, 1885–89), 267–68; (41) L. Wouters, C.Ss.R., *De virtute castitatis et de vitiis oppositis* (Bruges: Beyaert, 1932), nos. 111–12; (42) M. Zalba, S.J., *Theologiae moralis summa* 3 (Madrid: B.A.C., 1958), nos. 1514–18.

supervised from Rome, suffices to explain the harmony of action.[52]

We think this opinion is correct. Moreover, some decisions of the Holy See and some statements of national hierarchies both refer to the approved authors of the theological manuals and subsequently are referred to in later editions of the manuals. This situation is a paradigm case of the ordinary Magisterium of the Church, dispersed throughout the world, agreeing in one judgment and universally proposing it as if with one voice.

Sixth, when the statements of Pius XI and Pius XII summed up and reaffirmed this existing consensus, there was no significant negative reaction within the Catholic Church. Not only did the bishops readily accept the teaching of *Casti connubii*, but many actively took part in an effort to carry out its program by encouraging family-life movements, by instructing and directing their own clergy, and by making public statements repeating the teaching when such statements seemed called for.

These considerations, we believe, make clear that the received Catholic teaching on the morality of contraception was *universally* proposed by Catholic bishops

[52] Noonan, *Contraception*, 431–32. Noonan's analyses (397–405 and 415–19) of the responses of the Holy See emphasize their incidental differences with respect to cooperation, interrogation, and so on, thus obscuring the central point that every one of these responses says or takes for granted that the contraceptive acts in question are objectively grave matter (see Ford and Kelly, *Contemporary Moral Theology*, 2:258–60).

in communion with one another and with the successor of Peter. Bishops and Popes personally repeated the teaching in official acts, and by their authority they guided, supported, and endorsed the teaching by way of the seminaries in its direct application in pastoral practice.

But if the teaching was universal and even authoritative, was it proposed authoritatively as a point *to be held definitively*? The following considerations show that it was. First, a negative point. We know of no evidence—and Noonan points to none—that anyone handed on the received teaching as if it were a private opinion, a merely probable judgment, or a commendable ideal which the faithful might nevertheless blamelessly choose to leave unrealized. The teaching always was proposed as a received and certain part of the obligatory moral teaching of the Church.

Second, the teaching is that acts intended to impede procreation are in species gravely evil—that is, are the matter of mortal sin. This fact—which was pivotal in the argument for the binding force of the Tradition which we quoted in section I—makes clear the unqualified character of the intellectual assent demanded for the teaching.[53] When the Church proposes a moral teaching as one that Christians must try to follow if they

---

[53] In section II we pointed out that Kleutgen's commentary on Vatican I's second schema *De ecclesia* makes a case for infallibility in the moral teaching of the Magisterium, even assuming such teaching extends to points in no way contained in revelation. One of Kleutgen's arguments (Mansi 53, 327C) turns upon the precise point of the gravity of the Church's judgments in her moral teaching.

are to be saved, she a fortiori presents the teaching as one which must be accepted as certain. The Magisterium permitted no differing opinions about the morality of contraception, and so probabilism was inapplicable. Thus the conditions under which the teaching was proposed left no room for doubt in the matter.

Third, the insistent repetition of the received teaching in recent times when it was called into question outside the Catholic Church often included and always implied the proposition that this is an obligatory teaching, one which every Catholic must hold even though it is denied by other Christians.

Fourth, the teaching on the morality of contraception often was proposed as a moral norm divinely revealed. Since it was proposed as revealed, a fortiori it was proposed as a teaching *to be held definitively*. We prescind from the question whether the evidence alleged to show that the condemnation of contraception is divinely revealed does or does not show this. The point we wish to make is simply this: When one who is proposing a teaching appeals to divine revelation to confirm the truth of what he proposes, he implicitly calls for an assent of divine faith and thus proposes the teaching as one to be held definitively.

Very often those who proposed the received Catholic teaching on contraception explicitly appealed to Sacred Scripture. In making this explicit appeal—when both those who were teaching and those who were taught regarded the passage cited as the revealed word of God—those who made it clearly implied that the teaching proposed was divinely revealed.

The passage most often explicitly cited was Genesis 38:9–10, concerning Onan. As we have said, we prescind from the question of what this passage shows. Whatever one thinks it shows, the fact is that this passage was often cited to support the teaching that contraception is gravely evil. Those who used the passage often clearly proposed the teaching for belief as divinely revealed.

In a symposium conducted after the publication of *Humanae vitae*, Msgr. Joseph Coppens, an Old Testament scholar, made the point we are making:

> The role of the personal authority of the pope seems to be sometimes exaggerated. As I see it the pope's main argument is not based in first instance upon the guidance of the Spirit in his personal case, but upon the position that the teaching of the encyclical is *constans ecclesiae doctrina*. All moral textbooks, theological and philosophical, from the earliest centuries on, speak of Onan's sin as contraception. (Whether this agrees with contemporary scholarship, which sees Onan's sin as a refusal to obey the levirate law, is not at issue here.) Onan's sin has been constantly and universally condemned; this is the constant teaching referred to in the encyclical.[54]

Undoubtedly, Coppens overstated the extent to which appeal was made to the text on Onan.[55] But it was

---

[54] Joseph Coppens, in "A Symposium on 'Humanae vitae' and the Natural Law", *Louvain Studies* 2 (Spring 1969): 224.

[55] But it was appealed to very frequently; see Noonan, *Contraception*, 97–98, 101, 137–38, 139 (n. 35), 161–62, 225–26, 234, 298, 343, 359, 360, 361 (n. 38), 364, 367, 374, 403, 405, 420, 423, and 427. See also our next two footnotes.

very widely used, especially during the nineteenth and twentieth centuries, when "onanism" and "conjugal onanism" became the standard expressions in the theological literature for contraception as such. Many authors used Genesis 38:9–10 as a proof text for the teaching condemning all positive acts intended to impede procreation; some authors explicitly stated that this text showed that God himself, as Author of nature and supreme Lawgiver, condemned the sin as mortal.[56] Several other authors simply note that the sin of contraception is named from Onan's act and refer to the passage, leaving the reader to draw his own conclusions.[57]

Authors who do not cite the text almost always fall into one of two categories: Either they set forth moral norms briefly with no theological arguments to support them, or they systematically use only certain theological loci, such as statements by other theologians or statements of the Magisterium. Only a few theologians mention the text on Onan and forbear to use it because of doubts about its relevance; while they agree in condemning all contraceptive acts as gravely

---

[56] Of the authors listed in our n. 51, those numbered as follows in one way or another invoke the authority of Gen 38:9–10: 1, 2, 3, 4, 5, 8, 10, 11, 12, 14, 15, 17, 18, 20, 22, 25, 26, 27, 29, 30, 31, 32, 35, 36, 37, and 40. The following, while they reject contraception as gravely evil regardless of the method, take "onanism" in a narrow sense and so perhaps only regard the passage as relevant to *coitus interruptus*: 2, 5, 14, 15, 22, 29, 31, 32, and 40.

[57] The following refer to Gen 38:9–10 for the *name* of the sin: 13, 28, 33, 34, and 42.

evil, they offer other grounds for the condemnation.[58]

In the same symposium from which we have quoted, Coppens also referred to Romans 1:26–27 as a source of the constant teaching. Again we prescind from the question of what this passage shows. Moreover, in this case the text was not often *explicitly* appealed to in support of the condemnation of contraception. However, contraception often was condemned as a sin against nature; it was rejected as evil inasmuch as it is contrary to the natural use of marriage.[59] This characterization of contraception, by those who believed it revealed in Romans 1:26–27 that it is gravely sinful to exchange the natural for an unnatural use, implied that it is revealed that contraception is gravely sinful.

Two other ways of categorizing acts intended to impede procreation also imply that it is revealed that such acts are gravely evil—namely, the characterization of contraceptive acts as homicide[60] and as adul-

---

[58] The following refer to Gen 38:9–10 but forbear to rely on its authority: 23, 38, and 39.

[59] See Noonan, *Contraception*, 131, 172–73, 215, 223–27, 242, 260–61, 357, and 366–68. It also seems to us that the widespread use of the "perverted-faculty argument" is explained less by its contribution to rational clarification of the received teaching than by its evocation of the perversity of contraception as against the natural use of marriage.

[60] Ibid., 91–94, 98–99, 100–101, 146, 155, 160, 167, 168, 172–78, 232–37, and 360–65. It must be recalled that *Si aliquis* stipulated that contraceptive acts be held as homicide. We regard the assimilation of contraception to homicide as a sound insight. Contraception does not attack an existing human life, indeed, but it is an expression of a heart set against the beginning of a new life; for the contraceptive

tery.⁶¹ From the Sermon on the Mount and the *Didache* down to today, Christians have used the Ten Commandments as a framework to be authentically developed by expansion and deepening for their own moral formation. To call contraceptive acts "homicide" or "anticipated homicide" or "quasi homicide" or "interpretively homicide" was to assimilate them to a species of acts everyone believed to be condemned by divinely given moral law and so was implicitly to propose the condemnation of contraception as revealed. The same is true when contraceptive acts were characterized as adulterous.

If one considers the explicit appeals made to Genesis 38:9–10 together with the implicit appeals made to the same passage, to Romans 1:26–27, and to the Ten Commandments, one realizes that most who handed on the Catholic teaching on contraception claimed the authority of Scripture, which they believed to be the authority of divine revelation, in support of this teaching. Whether one thinks this claim was valid or not—a question we are not considering here—no one can deny that those who made it proposed the teaching on behalf of which they made it as a moral norm *to be held definitively*.

---

act in and of itself does nothing but intervene against human life in the moment in which it would be passed on. See Germain Grisez, "A New Formulation of a Natural-Law Argument against Contraception", *Thomist* 30 (1966): 343–61.

⁶¹ See Noonan, *Contraception*, 136–37, 174–77, and 372; this interpretation of the malice of contraception was spread by the use of *Aliquando* by both Gratian and Peter Lombard.

The great papal statements of Pius XI, Pius XII, and Paul VI are best understood in the light of the previous teaching of the Magisterium. These papal statements repeat, articulate, share in, and contribute to the handing on of the teaching by the ordinary Magisterium. When the Popes dealt with the question of contraception, it already was an old question, not a new one. They reaffirmed an established Christian moral norm.

Pius XI condemns contraception as a sin against nature. He claims that Holy Writ bears witness that God pursues with the greatest detestation this abominable crime; having made this claim, he uses Saint Augustine's exegesis of Genesis 38:9–10 to support it.[62] He also invokes the constancy of the Tradition, saying that the Christian doctrine on contraception was handed down without interruption from the very beginning. He speaks on behalf of the Catholic Church, as God's ambassador, and thus claims to restate nothing other than the demand of God's will, which must be accepted as a condition of salvation.[63]

Pius XII officially summarizes the teaching of Pius XI. In doing so, he asserts that his predecessor solemnly proclaimed *anew*—thus making reference to

---

[62] It is important to note that Pius XI's appeal to the authority of Scripture is complete *before* his reference to Augustine and the latter's exegesis of Gen 38:9–10. The reference itself is a summoning of a witness and is hardly incidental, as was mistakenly alleged by some theological *periti* of the pontifical Commission for the Study of Problems of Population, Family, and Birthrate (Robert G. Hoyt, ed., *The Birth Control Debate* [Kansas City, Mo.: National Catholic Reporter, 1968], 63).

[63] *Casti connubii* (*AAS* 22 [1930], 559–60).

Tradition—the fundamental law governing the marital act. Pius XII also articulates the definitive character of the received teaching in a most emphatic way: "This teaching is as valid today as it was yesterday; and it will be the same tomorrow and always", thus applying to this point of moral teaching the unalterability that Hebrews 13:8 ascribes to Jesus Christ himself.[64]

Paul VI in *Humanae vitae* uses more cautious language. But his stance is the same as that of his two predecessors insofar as he also confirms the prior teaching of the ordinary and universal Magisterium. He states that the principles of the moral teaching on matrimony are "based on the natural law, illuminated and enriched by divine revelation" (section 4); some of the conclusions of the papal Commission for the Study of Problems of Population, Family, and Birthrate *could not* be accepted as final *mainly* because they diverged from "the moral doctrine on matrimony, proposed by the Magisterium of the Church with constant firmness" (section 6); married persons must conform to the creative plan of God, which "the constant teaching of the Church declares" (10); the relevant norms of natural law are interpreted by the constant teaching of the Church (11); the Church did not make and cannot change these norms, of which she is only the guardian and interpreter (18); the Church's teaching on contraception "promulgates the divine law" (20); the Church *hands down* these inviolable requirements of divine law (25); the received teaching

---

[64] "Address to the Midwives" (*AAS* 43 [1951], 843).

on contraception is part of the "saving teaching of Christ" (29).

None of these Popes says that the teaching he reaffirms has been proposed infallibly by the ordinary Magisterium. But their statements are not merely compatible with this position; they supply very important evidence in support of it; and, indeed, the substance and the manner of their statements are difficult to explain unless one supposes that these three Popes implicitly supposed—though not necessarily explicitly thought—that the position they reaffirmed is infallibly taught and hence is one to which the Catholic Church is unalterably committed.

We think the facts show as clearly as anyone could reasonably demand that the conditions articulated by Vatican II for infallibility in the exercise of the ordinary Magisterium of the bishops dispersed throughout the world have been met in the case of the Catholic Church's teaching on contraception. At least until 1962, Catholic bishops in communion with one another and with the Pope agreed in and authoritatively proposed one judgment to be held definitively on the morality of contraception: Acts of this kind are objectively, intrinsically, and gravely evil. Since this teaching has been proposed infallibly, the controversy since 1963 takes nothing away from its objectively certain truth. It is not the received Catholic teaching on contraception which needs to be rethought. It is the assumption that this teaching could be abandoned as false which needs to be rethought.

IV

The preceding argument raises a number of questions and is bound to draw certain objections. In this section we deal with a few of the more likely and the more important of these questions and objections.

The conditions for infallible teaching articulated by Vatican II make clear that if the Catholic teaching on contraception has been proposed infallibly, then this moral norm either is contained in divine revelation itself or has been proposed by the teaching Church because this was required for the Magisterium to fulfill its responsibility to guard as inviolable and expound with fidelity the deposit of divine revelation. This raises the question: Is the norm contained in divine revelation, and, if it is not, how is it connected with revelation?

We do not assert that the norm is divinely revealed. This question is one from which we have prescinded. Our position rather is this: If the norm is not contained in revelation, it is at least connected with it as a truth required to guard the deposit as inviolable and to expound it with fidelity. In support of this position, we first point out that no one has seriously tried to show that anything in revelation is *incompatible* with the Church's teaching on the morality of contraception. Admittedly, it does not seem there is any way to establish *conclusively* that this teaching either pertains to revelation or is connected with it apart from the fact that the ordinary Magisterium has proposed the teaching in the manner in which it has, and the faithful as a whole until recently have accepted the norm as binding.

But a similar state of affairs has been used as a basis for solemnly defining at least one dogma: that of the Assumption of the Blessed Virgin Mary.[65]

The next point we wish to make is that while we ourselves do not assert that the condemnation of contraception is revealed, it still is significant that most of those who handed down this teaching, in one way or another, more or less explicitly, *proposed* it as revealed.

Few today assert that there is an explicit condemnation of contraception in Genesis 38:9-10 or Romans 1:26-27 or that there is an implicit condemnation of it in the Ten Commandments. However, those who invoked these texts when they taught that contraceptive practices are forbidden by God did not interpret them in isolation from the whole body of Christian teaching. Christians grounded their moral insights more upon their meditation upon the whole of divine revelation— contained both in Scripture and in the concrete reality of Christian life—than upon an exact reading of isolated texts. Once in possession of these moral insights, and convinced that they formulated demands of God's will for Christian life, Christians implicitly or explicitly relied upon particular texts, using them as authoritative witnesses to the truth and the obligatory character of the moral norms which seemed to them to belong to the law of Christ.

Thus, exegetical arguments can go on forever, but

[65] In defining the dogma of the Assumption, Pius XII argues— "Munificentissimus Deus" (*AAS* 42 [1950] 757–69)—from the universality of the acceptance of the doctrine as a matter of faith to its objective status as a truth pertaining to divine revelation.

the fact remains that a great many Christian teachers and scholars who firmly believed that contraception is contrary to the will of God also were convinced that they could use Genesis 38:9–10 or some other text *as an illustration* of this moral norm. Perhaps those who used such a text as an illustration were mistaken in doing so. But if one bears in mind what they were doing, how can one be *certain* that they were mistaken? Even if the moral truth which was illustrated by such an appeal to Scripture is not itself revealed, still the use of Scripture to illustrate a teaching closely connected with revelation would not be inappropriate.

Furthermore, apart from the texts that are commonly used as illustrations, there are certain scriptural and historical data that suggest that contraception might have been rejected from the very beginning of Christianity. There are explicit rejections of *pharmakeia* in Galatians 5:20 and in Revelation 9:21, 21:8, and 22:15. *Pharmakeia*, often translated "sorcery" or "witchcraft", refers to the use of potions, including abortifacient and sterilizing drugs.[66] As Noonan points out, it is possible that these passages reflect the primitive Christian judgment on contraception. They might have been understood by their first readers as easily as the statement that the Church's teaching excludes use of the "pill" is

[66] See Noonan, *Contraception*, 44–45. Cf. *Didache* 2, 2a, and 5, 1c, where the context more clearly suggests that contraception is in question. Concerning the *Didache*, its antiquity and importance, see Robert M. Grant, ed., *The Apostolic Fathers,* vol. 3, *Barnabas and the Didache,* tr. Robert A. Kraft (New York: Nelson, 1965); the passages cited are annotated pp. 144 and 157.

understood today, even without mention of what the "pill" is and what it is used for.

There also is evidence in ancient Jewish writings which shows that Jews at the time of Christ rejected at least some methods of contraception.[67] Jesus did not abolish Jewish morality; he purified and restored it, deepened and transformed it into a new morality suited to those called to be children of God. If Scripture does not record the judgment of the primitive Church upon contraception, still such a judgment may well have been made, appropriating and refining an existing Jewish moral norm. In this way the received Catholic teaching on the morality of contraception could have been included in the earliest Christian moral instruction. There is no need to assume that all the details of moral instruction dating from apos-

[67] Noonan, *Contraception*, 49–54. Cf. David M. Feldman, *Birth Control in Jewish Law* (New York and London: NYU Press and University of London Press, 1968), 109–93. Although Feldman is procontraception, he carefully cites many basic and secondary sources which are anticontraception. The basic Talmudic texts, which record an earlier oral tradition, are *Yebamoth* 34b, *Niddah* 13a, and *Shabbath* 110b. These texts indicate there was near unanimity among the rabbis that male diversion of semen from procreation is forbidden (Gen 38:9–10 is understood in this sense); no one approved sterilization for either sex. The debate was whether women could use birth-control devices. Feldman's discussion of the Baraita of the "Three Women" (169–75), which specifies cases in which a married woman may (or must) use a *mokh*, shows that not all Jews maintained an *unqualified* condemnation of female protective devices, but this also indicates that a prima facie exclusion of contraception was taken for granted, since otherwise there would be no occasion to discuss exceptional cases.

tolic times are mentioned explicitly in the New Testament.

The preceding considerations could be used to argue that the condemnation of contraception might be included in revelation. But we prescind from the question of what is or might be revealed, and we use these considerations only to show how the norm excluding contraception might at least be connected with divine revelation.

A further consideration, we think, makes the connection even clearer. But this explanation must not be separated from the conclusion already reached: That the received Catholic teaching on contraception has been proposed infallibly by the ordinary Magisterium. We are here only answering a question raised by this conclusion, not trying to prove it again.

There is historical evidence of the explicit Christian condemnation of contraception in the face of Gnostic, Manichean, and pagan attitudes toward procreation, sex, marriage, and human life.[68] Noonan sets out this evidence, taking it to show that the "formation of the early Christian doctrine on contraception" was a *response* to these alien attitudes.[69]

But Noonan seems to forget that Christians were exposed to many conflicting stimuli, and their responses were not mere reflexes. The selective and differentiating responses which Christians worked out and put forth against alien morals should be understood as effects of their effort to be both creative and faithful.

---

[68] Noonan, *Contraception*, 56–139. [69] Ibid., 56.

Christ promised his followers that they would be taught by the Spirit to understand the fullness of the gospel; their responses must be evaluated in the light of this promise.

When all Christians reached and maintained one judgment upon some non-Christian attitude or practice, the principle of their response is manifest. It is their Christian heritage held in common. In other words, the Christian consensus on contraception is no accident, but a properly Christian judgment, clarified by the light of the Spirit teaching inwardly and grasped by a sense of faith already shaped by Christian teaching on the creative activity of God, on the value of human life, on the divine design of marriage, on the meaning of Christian parenthood, and on sexual morality. If the condemnation of contraception by the Fathers of the Church was not a restatement of primitive teaching but was a fresh initiative, as Noonan urges, then the formation of this teaching ought to be viewed as a *creative* response *faithfully developing* Christian moral teaching.

In preaching the gospel of Christ, the apostles promulgated in the pagan world a morality truly new to it in respect to creation and life, sin and death, sex and marriage, virginity and parenthood. Elements of this morality already existed in the pagan world, but the balanced and tightly integrated ensemble was truly new and distinctively Christian. Reflecting upon this new morality of Christ—which excludes homosexual acts, incest, fornication, and adultery—the Fathers of the Church were forced by advocates of contraception whom Noonan discusses to take a stand on the matter. Does contraception pertain to the new morality of Christ or does it pertain to the old *porneia* of the pagans? Christians took their stand on this matter, and the stand was so appropriate that they continued to agree in the judgment which was their initial response centuries after the stimulus had ceased. Moreover, despite their divisions, Orthodox and Protestant as well as Catholic Christians proposed the same teaching until the present century.

If this account of the formation of the early Christian doctrine on contraception is correct, then this doctrine must be regarded as an authentic development of prior Christian moral teaching which was directly rooted in revelation. Some theologians have held that in such a development what is implicitly revealed becomes explicit. But in prescinding from the question of what is revealed, we also have prescinded from this view. We hold that a judgment reached by such a development certainly is closely connected with revelation, inasmuch as it is a response required to guard the deposit as inviolable and to expound it with fidelity. This is the conclusion we draw from the foregoing account of the formation of the early Christian doctrine on contraception, as Noonan himself describes it. By no mere accident, the Fathers of the Church shared a common insight that only a rejection of contraception would be consonant with the maintenance and unfolding of the beliefs and practices which already had flowed from the gospel of Christ.[70]

---

[70] Although we make no attempt to show that the immorality of contraception is revealed—we prescind carefully and consistently

Someone might object that the received Catholic teaching on contraception has been proposed as a matter of natural law, that as such this moral norm falls within the province of human reason, and that it thus can have no such close connection with divine revelation. In support of this argument they might point out that the Popes themselves distinguish and contrast the law of the gospel and natural law. For example, in *Humanae vitae* 4, Paul VI asserts the competence of the Magisterium in the matter of birth regulation, insofar as the Church is the guardian and interpreter of the moral law, "not only of the evangelical law, but also of the natural".

This objection is based upon a misunderstanding. "Natural law" has been referred to in the documents of the Magisterium mainly during the nineteenth and twentieth centuries; the principal use of the expression is to emphasize the objectivity of moral law in contrast with all positive law, even positive divine legislation.[71] Moreover, the Popes who have talked most about "natural law" have made it clear that human knowledge of such moral norms in fact depends very heavily upon

---

from this question—it must be confessed that if we were asked to show from the sources of revelation that this moral norm is somehow revealed, we would consider this an easier task than to show from the same sources that the doctrines of the Immaculate Conception and the Assumption are revealed. That these latter are revealed has been defined as a matter of faith. Perhaps only such a definition would ever settle the question whether the norm forbidding contraception is revealed (as against "connected with revelation").

[71] Josef Fuchs, S.J., *Natural Law: A Theological Investigation* (New York: Sheed & Ward, 1965), 10–13.

divine revelation; for many of these norms are revealed, while those which are not still fall within the competence of the Magisterium precisely insofar as it has the responsibility to teach mankind all that is necessary for salvation.[72]

Thus recent theories of natural law have no bearing upon the substance of the Catholic teaching on contraception or upon the status of any teaching as one which has been proposed as revealed or as closely connected with revelation. It is farfetched at best to try to argue from the Magisterium's use of the language of natural law to the conclusion that the Magisterium cannot be exercised infallibly in teaching on moral issues such as contraception.

It also is worth noting that the language used both by Vatican II and by Paul VI is consonant with and even strongly suggests that the Church's teaching on contraception belongs properly to what is required to guard the deposit of revelation as inviolable and to expound it with fidelity. Paul VI, as we noted above, refers in *Humanae vitae* 4 to the principles of the Church's moral teaching on matrimony as "based on the natural law, illuminated and enriched by divine revelation". Vatican II states in *Gaudium et spes* 50, specifically in reference to birth regulation, that couples must conform their consciences to the divine law,

---

[72] See *Humanae vitae*, 4, and the documents cited in its n. 1, especially *Magnificate dominum* (*AAS* 46 [1954]: 671–72); see also Thomas Aquinas, *Summa theologiae* 1–2, q. 99, a. 2; q. 100, a. 1; q. 106, a. 1; Fuchs, *Natural Law*, 144–62; John J. Reed, S.J., "Natural Law, Theology, and the Church", *TS* 26 (1965): 47–56.

"docile to the magisterium of the Church, which authoritatively interprets that law under the light of the gospel". And, as we noted above, in article 51 of the same constitution, the Council states that children of the Church may not use methods of regulating birth "which are disapproved of by the magisterium of the Church in its explaining of the divine law".

This brings us to another important question. Since we admit that the Catholic teaching on contraception might have been a development from more basic Christian teachings, how can one be sure that the controversy within the Church since 1963 does not portend a further development, which might safeguard the same goods which Christians have always prized while permitting particular contraceptive acts within the context of a marriage on the whole open to responsible parenthood?

Immediately after the paragraph which we quoted near the beginning of section III concerning the universality of the received Catholic teaching on contraception, Noonan goes on to suggest that the apparent fixity of the teaching might not be real. He introduces this suggestion as follows:

> The teaching, however, has not been proposed without reasons. It has not been unrelated to other doctrinal propositions. It has not been isolated from the environment in which Christians live. If the teaching were constant while the reasons, related doctrine, and environment changed, it would not be the same teaching

that these reasons, doctrine, and environment now supported.[73]

One of the documents of the pontifical Commission for the Study of Problems of Population, Family, and Birthrate suggested that a papal document on responsible parenthood should embrace the theory of development that Noonan had proposed. The real position proposed by the Magisterium until now would not be abandoned, this schema claimed, if the Church were

---

[73] Noonan, *Contraception*, 6. While we disagree with Noonan's conclusion that the Catholic Church today can contradict what Catholics universally believed and taught concerning the morality of contraception until the present controversy, we give Noonan full credit for establishing what was believed and taught and for showing what various documents meant in their concrete historical contexts. Apart from a few points, we do not disagree with Noonan about facts and interpretations. We do disagree with him about the truth of the received teaching. Someone might suppose that we could not deny Noonan's conclusion without carrying out a work similar to his, establishing a history incompatible with his, and thus refuting Noonan's premises. But this supposition would be sound only if Noonan's conclusion were entailed deductively by the premises. It is not; it follows as a hypothesis from an inductive argument. The *addition* (to the premises Noonan himself establishes) of a proposition he did not consider—the proposition affirmed by Vatican II concerning the infallibility of the ordinary Magisterium under certain conditions—leads us to a conclusion contradictory to Noonan's. His own work provides the evidence, including the indispensable interpretation of texts in historical contexts, that the conditions specified by Vatican II did obtain in the case of the Church's teaching on contraception. If anyone should simply reassert Noonan's conclusion in reply to our argument, without offering fresh support for Noonan's thesis and directly rebutting our argument, he would simply beg the question against us.

to approve the use of *some* contraceptive means—ones "human and decent, ordered to favoring fecundity in the totality of married life and toward the realization of the authentic values of a fruitful matrimonial community". For what the Tradition always upheld, it was argued, were two values: procreation and the rectitude of marital intercourse. And what the Tradition always condemned was a contraceptive intervention with motives spoiled by egoism and hedonism.[74]

Formally, Noonan's statement "If the teaching were constant . . . it would not be the same teaching" appears to be a contradiction in terms. Even if the sentence is interpreted in a way that permits it to be coherent, it is neither obvious in itself nor justified by what precedes it. In his book as a whole, Noonan does not even try to show that the Catholic Church's teaching *on contraception* was not the same in the early 1960s as in the previous decades and centuries. Rather, he shows that reasons for the Church's teaching, related doctrines, and the environment have changed, and thus he tries to show that the teaching itself need not be regarded as fixed forever but rather as a changeable expression of fundamental values.

The problem of the development of doctrine is a complex one. We certainly do not wish to deny that there can be and has been genuine development of Catholic teaching on many subjects, including marital morality. We do not claim that genuine development

---

[74] An English translation of this document is in Hoyt, *Birth Control Debate*, 88–90.

must be limited to the mere explication of consequences already entailed by truths always believed. However, we do maintain that no genuine development in the Church's teaching, once it has been infallibly proposed, can *contradict* what was previously proposed, properly understood in the sense in which it was proposed. If the Church infallibly proposed a teaching at one time and later proposed a contradictory teaching as an authentic development of its basic doctrine, then the Church's teaching would lose its meaning. An incoherent succession of statements cannot form a unified process in which identity is maintained through progress; contradiction would end the Tradition of faith, not guard it as inviolable and expound it with fidelity.[75]

[75] Cf. DS 1797–1800, 1817–18 (3017–20, 3042–43). We are aware of more radical conceptions of development which have been advanced; see Nicholas Lash, *Change in Focus: A Study of Doctrinal Change and Continuity* (London: Sheed & Ward, 1973), 143–82. The inevitable difficulty with any theory which allows a *proposition* (not the verbal formula but the meaning of the language used) once infallibly taught to be contradicted is that there is no objective criterion remaining by which to limit such "development". Once the objective conditions of incarnational Christianity are set aside, one must fall back upon some sort of subjective gnosis, e.g., "religious experience" and its interpretation by a consensus of contemporary theologians. But while there is some consensus about what is to be abandoned, there is little consensus about what is to be retained. Even where there is some consensus, the ordinary Christian who once admits "developments" which contradict received teachings is hardly likely to be impressed by an esoteric clique of professional interpreters of contemporary awareness. Thus, to admit a teaching contradictory to one infallibly proposed, even on a matter of comparatively low status in the hierarchy of truths of faith, is to end the handing on of the deposit, not to guard it as inviolable and expound it with fidelity.

Catholic teaching on marital morality always has upheld the values of procreation and the rectitude of marital intercourse, and it has rejected egoistic and hedonistic motives for engaging in sexual intercourse. However, we deny that this is the whole sum and substance of the teaching proposed by the ordinary and universal Magisterium on the morality of contraception. The position proposed universally as an obligatory norm involved certain recurrent propositions: "The teachers of the Church have taught without hesitation or variation that certain acts preventing procreation are gravely sinful", as Noonan sums up the matter in the paragraph in which he outlines the universality of the received teaching. To exclude ambiguity, we need only add that the teachers of the Church have never taught that *any* acts intended to prevent procreation are permissible or in themselves only venially sinful.

Apart from the recurrent *propositions* condemning the use of contraceptives as such, it would be difficult, if possible at all, to discern the *values* which the Tradition has always upheld and the attitudes it has always condemned. Certainly, no teacher of the Church prior to 1963 ever said that contraceptive acts are gravely sinful *insofar as* or *on condition that* they do not favor fecundity in the totality of married life and are not directed to the values of fruitful matrimonial community. Furthermore, while it was considered blameworthy to engage in intercourse with egoistic or hedonistic motives—for example, having intercourse for pleasure *alone*—such defects in motivation were not considered to vitiate marital intercourse to the extent of making it gravely sinful, unless the person wishing to satisfy his sexual desire *did something*—such as giving a drink or doing something else so that a man could not generate or a woman conceive or offspring be born, as *Si aliquis* puts it.

Moreover, the consensus of approved theological authors of modern times makes unmistakably clear what an unbiased reading of the Tradition already indicates: Contraceptive acts are condemned as intrinsically evil. The teaching of the Magisterium did not condemn contraceptive acts for the motives with which or the circumstances in which they were done. In fact, even the contraceptive acts of a poor woman motivated by the difficulty of feeding her children were explicitly condemned as grave sins—though not as grave as similar acts of one in other circumstances and with other motives—by Burchard of Worms in his *Decretum* (around 1010).[76] It is pure fantasy to suppose that the Church's moral teaching was based upon a weighing and balancing of values; for such a consequentialist calculus is altogether alien to the Christian Tradition, which always has been absolutist with respect to fundamental moral norms, such as those bearing upon sexual behavior and the killing of the innocent.

In his book Noonan organizes and interprets the data of history, working out a many-stranded case in favor of his view that the Church could develop her perennial teaching on marital morality by accepting contraception

---

[76] Noonan, *Contraception*, 160.

as moral. Among the many strands in this case, one is especially crucial: Noonan argues that the positive requirement of procreative purpose was an important part of the underpinning of the doctrine against contraception.[77] No one today supposes that marital intercourse without the intent to procreate is always sinful. Thus, Noonan thinks, the condemnation of contraception might also be reversed.

From our present vantage point, the first question is: Did the requirement of positive procreative purpose ever meet the conditions for the infallible exercise of the ordinary Magisterium articulated by Vatican II? The answer is clearly negative for the following reasons.

Some Fathers of the Church, including Augustine, Caesarius of Arles, and Gregory the Great, did teach that marital intercourse without intent to procreate is venially sinful.[78] But this teaching, although accepted and passed on by some other Catholic teachers, certainly never had the universality of the teaching against contraception. Moreover, even those who held that procreative purpose is necessary to render marital

[77] Ibid., 329 and passim.
[78] Ibid., 130–31 and 150. Noonan also shows (76–77) that Clement of Alexandria and certain other Fathers set down as the Christian ideal that husbands should seek intercourse "only for the raising up of children", without showing what guilt attached to failure to meet this ideal. Noonan also claims (79–81) Ambrose and Jerome as proponents of exclusive procreative purpose, but in the evidence he produces it is not clear that they are proposing a *moral norm* to be held definitively.

intercourse wholly blameless did not claim that violation of the requirement imperiled one's salvation.

To propose a norm excluding some kind of act as mortally sinful is to propose a teaching to be held definitively. To say that an act is venially sinful is not to say that a norm excluding it from Christian life is to be held definitively. This is especially true in respect to the Fathers of the Church, whose notion of the *venial* seems in many contexts to be broad enough to include much we would regard today not as a sin but only as a mistake or an imperfection or something in one way or another falling short of the ideal.

Noonan points to the use of certain Scripture texts, but the texts he adduces do not show that *procreative purpose* was alleged to be a divinely revealed requirement to free marital intercourse of sin; if they show anything, they show that some thought it divinely revealed that *marital intercourse*, even with procreative purpose, could not be free of sin.[79]

The second question to ask about the requirement of procreative purpose is whether Noonan is correct in thinking that this teaching, which is today considered erroneously narrow, goes far in explaining the origin and persistence of the Catholic teaching that contra-

[79] Thus Ps 50:7, "Behold I was conceived in sins, and in delights my mother bore me", in the quotation from Gregory cited by Noonan (151), hardly supports exclusive procreative purpose as the justification for intercourse. If Noonan's account (80–81) of Jerome's handling of the text of Tobias is correct, it does not show that Jerome appealed to Scripture to establish exclusive procreative intent as a divinely revealed norm but rather that he tampered with the text of Scripture while purporting to translate it.

ception is always wrong. Several considerations show that Noonan's argument on this matter fails.

First, he claims that the teaching of Gregory the Great would have rendered contraception unthinkable, although Gregory himself says nothing on the subject of contraception.[80] Second, Noonan offers no support at all for his intrinsically implausible supposition that the condemnation of contraception as a grave sin somehow followed from the exclusion as venial of intercourse without procreative intent. Third, to set up his argument about procreative purpose, Noonan relies upon a questionable analysis of what was meant by "rendering the debt". According to Noonan, "One spouse seeking and the other spouse returning was the model of marital relations accepted for analysis. That the theory of procreative purpose made one spouse a sinner, while the other fulfilled his duty, did not appear to the theologians as a weakness in theory."[81] On this analysis, Noonan argues that the great scholastic theologians, such as Saint Thomas and Saint Bonaventure, did not recognize that marital intercourse without procreative purpose can be good and holy for both partners.[82]

As a matter of fact, however, Saint Thomas explicitly states that marital intercourse in which the spouses render the debt *to each other* is totally excused from sin:

> Just as the goods of matrimony, insofar as they are present habitually [implicit in the consent], make

[80] Ibid., 150.   [81] Ibid., 284.
[82] Ibid., 193–99, 246–57, and 284–86.

marriage upright and holy, so also insofar as they are present in the actual intention, with regard to those two goods relevant to the act of marriage, they make the marital act upright. Accordingly, when spouses come together for the sake of procreating offspring, or so they may render the debt to each other, which pertains to fidelity, they are totally excused from sin.[83]

Aquinas' use of the plural throughout this passage shows that he is speaking of both spouses together; they are *totally* excused from sin when they *render the debt to each other*.[84] Saint Bonaventure similarly holds that marital affection is sufficient to excuse unbelievers from sin in their conjugal relations; in believers it not only excuses from sin but brings grace with the act.[85]

---

[83] *In Sent.* 4, dist. 31, q. 2, a. 2; cf. *In 1 ad Corinthios*, c. 7, lect. 1, a late work, in which Aquinas still distinguishes intercourse to render the debt from that to satisfy a desire which does not arise from concern about a marital good but nevertheless respects the limits of the marital bond.

[84] Noonan's interpretation of Saint Thomas' teaching on marital sex has been criticized in two studies: Germain G. Grisez, "Marriage: Reflections Based on St. Thomas and Vatican Council II", *Catholic Mind* 64 (June 1966): 4–19; Fabian Parmisano, O.P., "Love and Marriage in the Middle Ages, II", *New Blackfriars* 50 (1969): 649–60. In "Love and Marriage in the Middle Ages, I", *New Blackfriars* 50 (1969): 599–608, Parmisano shows that the "new" theory, which Noonan credits (306–12) to Martin le Maistre (1432–81), was anticipated by Nicole Oresme (ca. 1320–82) without eliciting the reaction one would expect if a novel view were being put forward, especially since Oresme wrote in the vernacular and was a cleric—in fact, a bishop during the last few years of his life.

[85] Bonaventure, *In Sent.* 4, dist. 39, a. 1, q. 1; cf. q. 3; also dist. 26, a. 2, q. 3.

Noonan ignores such statements because he is diverted by a different question, which is usually treated in commentaries on the *Sentences*: Whether conjugal intercourse *to avoid fornication* is wholly without sin. Noonan refers to Saint Thomas' and Saint Bonaventure's treatments of this question when he alleges that they require procreative purpose on the part of spouses to clear both of them of sin.[86] Aquinas and Bonaventure do maintain that in this case only the partner who responds is blameless. There is something a bit excessive in the sexual desire of a Christian who demands intercourse of a spouse because the alternative is to succumb to the temptation to seek sexual satisfaction elsewhere. But neither Aquinas nor Bonaventure supposes that this case is typical of marital intercourse in which spouses faithfully give each other what is due in marriage, acting with marital affection.

Thus the argument that a now discarded requirement of conscious procreative purpose explains the persistence of the condemnation of contraception among the great scholastic theologians fails, for they simply did not hold this requirement.

After he published his book on contraception, Noonan went on to publish articles arguing as follows: The Church once condemned the taking of interest (usury) just as severely as it condemned contraception, but the Church now approves the taking of interest;

---

[86] Noonan, *Contraception*, 248, with n. 20. We have not examined other authors Noonan claims in support of his thesis, but it might be worthwhile to check all of them, bearing in mind that "fidelity" has a positive aspect and that "rendering the debt" can be mutual.

hence, the Church also can change its teaching on the morality of contraception.[87] Many others have articulated a similar argument. Once more the question is whether the condemnation of the taking of interest, insofar as this teaching has been changed, ever met the conditions for the infallible exercise of the ordinary Magisterium articulated by Vatican II. The answer is clearly negative for the following reasons.

As has often been argued by Catholic students of the matter, the teaching of Scripture and of the Fathers forbids charging interest on loans to the poor and condemns the greed and avarice of usurers, but this teaching does not deal with the taking of interest as such and does not envisage a situation in which moderate rates of interest are established by money markets. The decrees of the councils and Popes up to 1450 are aimed at the same evils attacked in Scripture and by the Fathers.[88]

In his study of scholastic theories of usury, published prior to the beginning of the debate among Catholics on contraception, Noonan himself rejected the view that the central Catholic teaching on the morality of the taking of interest had changed:

---

[87] The version on which our summary is based is John T. Noonan, Jr., "Authority, Usury and Contraception", *Cross Currents* 16 (Winter 1966): 71–75.

[88] See A. Vermeersch, S.J., "Usury", *Catholic Encyclopedia* 15 (New York: Appleton, 1912), 235–38, and the works cited by him; Thomas F. Divine, S.J., *Interest: An Historical and Analytical Study in Economics and Modern Ethics* (Milwaukee: Marquette University, 1959), 5–11, 24–35, and 45–64.

Moreover, as far as dogma in the technical Catholic sense is concerned, there is only one dogma at stake. Dogma is not to be loosely used as synonymous with every papal rule or theological verdict. Dogma is a defined, revealed doctrine taught by the Church at all times and places. Nothing here meets the test of dogma except this assertion, that usury, the act of taking profit on a loan without a just title, is sinful. Even this dogma is not specifically, formally defined by any pope or council. It is, however, taught by the tradition of the Church, as witnessed by papal bulls and briefs, conciliar acts, and theological opinion. This dogmatic teaching remains unchanged. What is a just title, what is technically to be treated as a loan, are matters of debate, positive law, and changing evaluation. The development on these points is great. But the pure and narrow dogma is the same today as in 1200.[89]

Although Noonan's formulation of his point here is neither completely satisfactory nor precise, his idea is clear: The moral teaching on the taking of interest proposed infallibly by the ordinary Magisterium has not changed.

The key to clarity in this matter is precision with respect to the concept of that usury which the Church condemns. The sin of usury is not simply the charging of interest on a loan, but the charging of interest on a loan *in virtue of the loan itself*, rather than in virtue of some factor related to the loan which provides a basis for demanding fair compensation. Thus, the Fifth

---

[89]John T. Noonan, Jr., *The Scholastic Analysis of Usury* (Cambridge, Mass.: Harvard University, 1957), 399–400.

Lateran Council (1515) explained what is forbidden: "For this is the proper interpretation of usury: when one seeks to acquire gain from the use of a thing which is not fruitful, with no labor, no expense, and no risk on the part of the lender."[90] Undoubtedly, there were many weighty statements by Catholic teachers, some of which shared in the authority of the Magisterium, which lacked the precision of the Fifth Lateran Council's definition of "usury". However, even if we grant that such statements were more or less seriously mistaken, such errors would not argue for the mutability of the received Catholic teaching on contraception, since the latter teaching is what is constant and universal amidst changes in the arguments given for it, teachings incidentally related to it (such as the view that intercourse without procreative purpose is venially sinful), and the cultural conditions in which Christians have lived.[91]

We expect that many other objections based upon alleged changes in the Church's moral teachings will be educed by critics of our argument. Many such objections have been put forward over and over again by

[90] DS 738 (1442).

[91] Also, Christian morality emphasizes goods that are intrinsic to persons, e.g., life and its beginnings, truth, justice, and holiness. By virtue of the Incarnation, such goods somehow take on a divine worth in respect to every human person, and these goods of our nature are destined for eternity, as Vatican II teaches (*Gaudium et spes*, 22, 27, and 39). The very nature of instrumental goods such as money can change, but the goods intrinsic to persons are not mutable as instrumental goods are. Money is a human institution; sex is a divine institution.

those who denied, questioned, or sought to restrict as much as possible the Church's infallibility, and these objections have been answered over and over again by Catholic apologists. As we said above in section I, we assume the infallibility of the Church here, both in general and in the particular case of the ordinary Magisterium under the conditions articulated by Vatican II. Still, it might be worthwhile to recall in outline the strategy which the apologist will use in dealing with all such objections, whether they are intended to attack the infallibility of the teaching Church in defining doctrines or in universally proposing a matter of faith or morals as a point to be held definitively.

In some cases it appears that a teaching infallibly proposed has subsequently been changed. But whatever change is authoritatively admitted by the Church does not go so far as to contradict what was formerly infallibly proposed, understood in the precise sense in which it was proposed. In other cases a teaching was proposed with some authority by the ordinary Magisterium and was later contradicted; but the teaching contradicted was never proposed infallibly, since it was neither solemnly defined nor proposed by the ordinary Magisterium in a manner which fulfilled the conditions articulated by Vatican Council II. For example, some members of the Magisterium might have proposed something to be held definitively, but at no time did the bishops dispersed throughout the world agree in their judgment. Or again, all of the members of the Magisterium might have agreed in one judgment and proposed it to the faithful, but not as a point to be held definitively, as happens at times in purely disciplinary matters or in the commending of some devotion.

In reviewing the history of Christian moral teaching, it is very important not to read the history backwards. It is possible for Christians today to see clearly that certain practices, attitudes, and institutions are incompatible with the law of Christ, although Christians in earlier centuries lacked insight into these matters. Looking back, it might appear that the Magisterium taught that these practices, attitudes, and institutions were upright and holy; considering them within their historical context, one sees that the situation was not so clear. The Magisterium presupposed and tacitly accepted in the past much which Christian sensitivity, stimulated both by exterior conditions and by the inner teaching of the Spirit, now can recognize as unacceptable. This fact does not show that the teaching Church earlier provided false guidance but only that the Church is now able to provide guidance on matters regarding which it was not prepared to make a judgment in earlier times.

In the controversy over contraception and in the reaction to *Humanae vitae*, much was made of the dissenting views of those outside the Catholic Church who nevertheless hold fast to the gospel of Christ, and also of the sense of the Catholic faithful who think that the use of contraceptives is morally permissible and even holy. What is to be said about these data if, as we have argued, the condemnation of contraception has been infallibly proposed by the ordinary Magisterium?

The first thing to be said is that the opinions of those who are not in communion with the See of Peter do not count in determining the universality which is a criterion for the Church's infallibility in teaching. If the opinions of other Christians were to count, then every heretical opinion on every point of Christian teaching would become an element in the normative Tradition, and the incoherence of such a collection of opinions would reduce Catholic teaching to babble. This is neither to deny that Christians separated from the unity of the Catholic Church share in revealed truth nor to say that their opinions should be regarded as worthless. However, a Catholic will evaluate such opinions by the standard of the Church's teaching and learn from other Christians only what comports with Catholic teaching and contributes to its authentic development.

Moreover, it is important to recall that both Orthodox and Protestant Christians, although not in communion with Rome, did accept and hand on the same teaching on the morality of contraception, as well as on most other moral questions, which we still receive in the Catholic Church. Many such separated Christians still hold fast to the same moral principles even today. The handing on of the common Christian moral Tradition for many centuries after the authority of the Magisterium was rejected argues very strongly for the judgment that this teaching is integral to the Christian Tradition. Hence, when Catholic theologians who argue for the approval of contraception characterize as "Christian" the opinions of those who today abandon the common Christian Tradition in this matter—and often in many others—and invoke the authority of these opinions, they beg the question as to what is Christian and do so in favor of an opinion universally rejected by Christians until the present century.

The sense of the Catholic faithful, correctly understood, is a genuine witness to the faith of the Church. *Sensus fidelium* refers to a reality sometimes also called *sensus fidei, sensus ecclesiae*, and so on. This reality is the subjective and conscious side of living, Christian Tradition, by which Christians discern as if by instinct the beliefs and practices proper to Christian life and distinguish them from those which are alien. But this Christian sense is not independent of revelation, Tradition, and the Magisterium—the objective means God has chosen to communicate his truth and life to all nations until the end of time. The sense of faith provides no mystical and privileged access to divine things which would permit the opinions of the faithful at a given time *insofar as these opinions conflict with received teaching* to become a criterion by which to measure the truth of that teaching.[92]

Thus the opinions of Catholics who regard the use of contraceptives as morally permissible should not be considered an expression of the *sensus fidelium*. The

---

[92] On a right understanding of *sensus fidelium*, see Yves M.-J. Congar, O.P., *Tradition and Traditions: An Historical and Theological Essay* (New York: Macmillan, 1967), 314–21; *The Meaning of Tradition* (New York: Hawthorn, 1964), 74–78; J. R. Geiselmann, *The Meaning of Tradition* (Freiburg: Herder, 1966), 19–23; J. P. Mackey, *The Modern Theology of Tradition* (New York: Herder and Herder, 1963), 95–122.

sensus fidelium remains a strong and effective witness in the Church, but it is to be found in those many other Catholics, including married couples, who remain firmly convinced that their salvation depends upon their doing their best to live up to Catholic moral teaching on this as on other matters. In this conviction they remain in solidarity with the faithful down through the ages who have accepted this norm for their conduct in marriage, struggled to live up to it, and accused themselves of grave sin when they failed to do so.

One final point is well worth noting in respect to the sense of the faithful. Ordinary Catholics have shown and continue to show a genuine Catholic sense by the manner in which they talk about the controversy over contraception. Whether inclined to one or to the other side of the controversy, ordinary Catholics spontaneously refer to the received teaching as "the teaching of the Church" and they refer to any acceptance of methods of birth regulation forbidden up to now as "a change in the Church's teaching".[93] Only those who are intellectually subtle and who are careful how they speak say that the received teaching is the "Roman principle" or the "papal teaching" or the "rule laid

---

[93] To consider how the faithful speak, not what they want, as evidence of the *sensus fidelium* is in line with the view of John Henry Newman, who insists (*On Consulting the Faithful in Matters of Doctrine*, ed. John Coulson [New York: Sheed & Ward, 1961], 54–55, 63, and 102–3) that by "consulting" the faithful he does not mean asking their advice but rather ascertaining the *fact* of their belief as a witness to the traditional teaching.

down in *Casti connubii*" and suggest that the acceptance of contraceptive methods of birth control by the Church would be a "genuine development" of the Church's teaching on marital morality and a "deepening" of the understanding of Christian faith.

Moreover, many of those Catholics who have decided to act contrary to the teaching of the Church on contraception remain deeply troubled about what they regard as Paul VI's failure to approve this practice. While such Catholics very often rely upon dissenting theological opinion in shaping their conduct, their consciences are not wholly at rest. Their *sensus fidei* persists in making its dissonant claim. One motive of theologians who publicly dissented from *Humanae vitae* was the laudable desire to try to help Catholics who in the course of the controversy had committed themselves wholeheartedly to the use of contraceptives. The still-troubled consciences of Catholics who practice contraception and even their drifting away from the Church provide testimony—testimony at once paradoxical, powerful, and sad—of their genuine *sensus ecclesiae*, which the dissenting opinion of theologians has failed either to alter or reduce to silence.

V

In this section we clarify the relationship between the argument we propose and defend in the present paper and the argument that was proposed in the pontifical Commission for the Study of Problems of Population,

Family, and Birthrate by those theologians who believed that the constant teaching of the Church on the morality of contraception could not be changed. The first point we wish to make is that the argument we are proposing now is compatible with the argument which one of the present authors together with other theological *periti* of the papal Commission proposed in 1966.

In May 1966 the theological *periti* of the Commission were asked by its secretary to draw up two summary documents, one briefly articulating the view of those who regarded the received teaching as unchangeable and the other briefly articulating the opposite view. These documents were intended for the internal use of the Commission, whose members—a group of sixteen cardinals and other bishops—were to meet in June. One of the present authors helped draw up the former of these documents, *Status quaestionis: Doctrina ecclesiae ejusque auctoritas*, which included an argument meant to show why the Church cannot change its answer to the question whether contraception always is gravely evil.

This argument developed the consideration, quoted in section I of the present paper, with respect to the binding force of the Tradition:

> The Church cannot change the answer *since this answer is true*. Whatever may be the possibility of a more perfect formulation of the teaching or perhaps of its genuine development, there is no possibility that the teaching itself is other than substantially true. It is true because the Catholic Church, instituted by Christ to show men

the sure road to eternal life, could not err so atrociously through all the centuries of its history. The Church cannot substantially err in teaching a very serious doctrine of faith or morals through all the centuries—even through one century—a doctrine constantly and insistently proposed as one necessarily to be followed in order to attain eternal salvation. The Church could not substantially err through so many centuries—even through one century—in imposing very heavy burdens under grave obligation in the name of Jesus Christ as it would have erred if Jesus Christ does not in fact impose these burdens. The Catholic Church could not in the name of Jesus Christ offer to the vast multitude of the faithful, everywhere in the world, for so many centuries an occasion of formal sin and spiritual ruin on account of a false doctrine promulgated in the name of Jesus Christ.

If the Church could err as atrociously as this, the authority of the ordinary magisterium in moral matters would be stultified; and the faithful henceforth could have no confidence in moral teaching handed down by the magisterium, especially in sexual questions.

The argument went on to emphasize that the question at issue was the *truth of the Church*'s teaching, not the *irreformability* of Pius XI's proclamation of this teaching in *Casti connubii*. Finally, the argument attempted to set aside, as irrelevant to the central issue, technical questions of fundamental theology. In particular, "In our discussion it is completely superfluous to argue subtly whether this teaching is technically 'infallibilis ex iugi magisterio'." The reason given is that if this teaching is not substantially true, then in moral matters the Magisterium itself will be seen to be completely superfluous.[94]

The main argument in the passage quoted above can be reformulated more briefly. No teaching which the Church proposes as a serious doctrine of faith or morals, necessarily to be followed in order to attain eternal salvation, and proposes universally through even one century, can be substantially in error. But the Church has proposed its moral teaching on contraception as an obligatory norm and a grave one, in the name of Christ, everywhere in the world, through many centuries. Therefore the Church could not err substantially in its teaching on contraception, and so the answer is true. Since the answer is true, the Church cannot change it.

Reformulated in this way, this argument clearly is an inadequately articulated version of the argument we have developed more adequately in sections II and III of the present paper. The 1966 argument uses the expression "the Church cannot err" but shies away from saying that the Church is infallible. It seemed, then, that to claim infallibility in the technical sense would be to invite a great deal of inconclusive argumentation about questions of fundamental theology and ecclesiology. In the present paper we have addressed ourselves to several of these questions.

Still, an inadequate articulation of a line of argument is not incompatible with a more adequate articulation of the same line of argument. Thus the argument we

---

[94] An English translation, which varies slightly from ours, appears in Hoyt, *Birth Control Debate*, 37–39.

propose now is not incompatible with the main argument proposed in 1966. However, the 1966 document also contained an attempt to set aside as not worthwhile in the circumstances the question whether the Church's teaching on contraception is infallibly taught by the ordinary Magisterium. We are now convinced it would have been better, if it had been possible, to attack this question; we are attempting by means of the present article to rectify the omission.

This brings us to our second point. Since the argument we are now proposing was not articulated in 1966, it was not considered and squarely answered by the theological *periti* of the papal Commission who believed change to be possible. Their theological working paper was entitled *Documentum syntheticum de moralitate regulationis nativitatum*. There are two passages in this document which are relevant to our present purpose.

First, its authors consider *Casti connubii*, rightly emphasizing that it should be considered in the context of the Tradition:

> The encyclical *Casti connubii* is of greater importance if it is considered as a particular contribution, a solemn one indeed, to the whole tradition, including the explicit official teaching of the past two centuries. For in this tradition contraceptive intervention never is approved, but always when the question arises it is reproved; this has occurred very often in recent centuries. But this tradition is in no way an apostolic tradition or an attestation of faith; rather, it is merely the tradition of a particular teaching formulated in diverse ways in diverse centuries.[95]

[95] Ibid., 64.

The theologians who wrote this document admit the existence of the Tradition. But in the absence of a clear and explicit argument showing the relevance of the facts, they simply assert without any argument at all that the Tradition is not a witness of faith. A possibility is ignored: That the Tradition, even if not an apostolic one, is a witness to faith in a truth closely connected with revelation, a truth infallibly proposed by the ordinary Magisterium. The theologians go on to summarize very compactly the main lines of Noonan's argument, emphasizing that changes had occurred in related teachings, in arguments for the received teaching, and in the situation.

The authors of *Documentum syntheticum* also answer the main argument put forward in *Status quaestionis*, which we quoted and discussed above. The answer formulated by the theologians who regard change as possible begins as follows:

> Not a few theologians and faithful fear that the very trust of the faithful in the magisterium in general could undergo damage on account of a changed teaching of the magisterium. For, they ask, how could the Holy Spirit permit in the Church such an error through so many centuries, even in these recent centuries, with so many consequences? However, the criteria for discerning what the Spirit can permit or not permit in the Church can hardly be determined a priori. We know a posteriori that there have been errors in the doctrine of the magisterium and of tradition. . . .

The argument goes on to use the example of the teaching on procreative purpose, along the lines this example was proposed by Noonan. The authors then note that there has been a tendency in recent decades to regard the noninfallible Magisterium as infallible in practice, while it must rather be expected that some mistakes occur in noninfallible teaching. They hold that in the matter of contraception there are very good reasons for doubt and reconsideration, and so change should not undermine confidence in the Magisterium; for this "change is really a step in a more mature grasp of the whole doctrine of the Church".[96]

Obviously, those who drafted this reply to the central argument of *Status quaestionis* missed what was intended to be the main thrust of the argument they wished to answer. The thrust of the argument in *Status quaestionis* was meant to be that the received Catholic teaching cannot be changed because it is true, and that one can be sure of its truth because the "Church could not substantially err" in proposing this moral norm, *considering the manner in which* the Church proposed it: to the whole world, as a serious teaching, acceptance of which is required for salvation. The reply in *Documentum syntheticum* shifted the focus to the concern about confidence of the faithful in the Magisterium, which the authors of *Status quaestionis* mentioned in a separate paragraph in what they meant to be a secondary argument.

Having shifted the focus of the argument, the authors of *Documentum syntheticum* beg the question at issue by assuming that the Church could be in substantial error

[96] Ibid., 67–68.

on the morality of contraception. That this assumption is question begging is shown by the fact that no reply is given to the contention of the argument in *Status quaestionis* that the *manner* of the Church's previous teaching on the particular matter in question precluded the possibility of error. Instead of coming to grips with this argument against the possibility of error in the particular case under consideration, the authors of *Documentum syntheticum* respond with the generality that one cannot tell in advance what the Spirit might permit, and that he has permitted the Church to make mistakes before.

Had the authors of *Status quaestionis* articulated more adequately their argument that the Church is irrevocably committed to the received moral teaching on contraception and made explicit the case for thinking that this teaching had been proposed infallibly by the ordinary Magisterium, then the generality with which the authors of *Documentum syntheticum* responded would have been patently question begging. For if a teaching has been proposed infallibly, whether it is defined or not, then there is a criterion determined a priori by Christ's promises as to what the Spirit will and will not permit: The Spirit will never permit the Church to contradict such a teaching.

As we have admitted, the authors of *Status quaestionis* can be faulted for not having made their argument more adequate and explicit and also for the distraction of the secondary argument in respect to the probable effect of a change upon confidence of the faithful in the Magisterium. Even so, a subsequent commentator—one by no means a partisan of the received teaching—easily set aside the distracting corollary, which he called a "political argument", and summarized with reasonable accuracy the main argument of *Status quaestionis*. He points out that one reason why the Pope rejected the argument for change surely is that the reply to the central argument of *Status quaestionis* in *Documentum syntheticum* simply "does not begin to look like a response to things as they are". If the argument in *Documentum syntheticum* for change "was to be accepted, it had to establish that such a thing was compatible with our faith in the Church; and it had also to recognize the consequences of admitting that it had in fact happened".[97]

Hans Küng, in his book on infallibility, interprets the argument of *Status quaestionis* as an attempt to show that the received teaching was infallibly proposed by the ordinary Magisterium. This interpretation, as we have shown, goes beyond the explicit intent of the authors of the 1966 document, but in the direction of the tendency implicit in the argument they proposed. Küng also observes, correctly we believe, that the authors of *Documentum syntheticum* did not come to grips with the argument against change:

> We can see now the real reason why the progressive majority of the commission were not able to convince the Pope. To judge from their own progressive report and the progressive official reaction of the commission,

[97] Michael Dummett, "The Documents of the Papal Commission on Birth Control", *New Blackfriars* 50 (1969): 243.

they had plainly not grasped sufficiently the full weight
of the argument of the conservative group: the moral
inadmissibility of contraception has been taught as a
matter of course and even emphatically by all bishops
everywhere in the world, in moral unity, unanimously,
for centuries and then—against opposition—in the present century up to the Council (and the confusion which
arose in this connection), as Catholic moral teaching to
be observed on pain of eternal damnation: it is therefore
to be understood in the light of the ordinary magisterium of pope and bishops as a factually *infallible* truth
of morals, even though it has not been *defined* as such.[98]

Although much of the argument in Küng's book has
been demolished by his critics,[99] they were dispensed
from dealing in depth with the point he makes in the
paragraph just quoted, since Küng fails to provide
exactly what the 1966 document itself failed to provide:
an adequate statement of the argument that the received
teaching has been proposed infallibly by the ordinary
Magisterium according to the criteria articulated by
Vatican II.

[98] Hans Küng, *Infallible? An Inquiry* (Garden City, N.Y.: Doubleday, 1971), 57–58. Although Küng proposes to replace infallibility
with indefectibility (181), he does not explain how errors in moral
teaching on the scale he assumes to have occurred can be reconciled
with indefectibility without this concept losing all meaning, not only
theoretically but also for the living of Christian life.

[99] See esp. Walter Brandmüller, "Hans Küng und die Kirchengeschichte: Kritische Anmerkungen zu seinem Buch *Unfehlbar?*" in
Karl Rahner, S.J., ed., *Zum Problem Unfehlbarkeit: Antworten auf die
Anfrage von Hans Küng* (Freiburg: Herder, 1971), 117–33, whose
critique seriously calls into question Küng's competence as a scholar.

In the documents of the papal Commission, besides the statements of the theological *periti* which we have been examining, there also was a schema drawn up by certain theologians, discussed by the cardinals and other bishops who were members of the Commission, amended to reflect this discussion and included in the final report of the Secretary of the Commission. This document is titled *Schema documenti de responsabili paternitate*. No response to the argument of *Status quaestionis* appears in this schema. Rather, it embraces the position, which we criticized in section IV, that the use of contraceptives could be approved today without really changing the traditional teaching.[100]

It is possible that the cardinals and bishops did not come to grips with the argument of *Status quaestionis* because they were unaware of the document. Cardinal Heenan, in an article published in May 1968, wrote that he had not seen the "minority report"—by which he meant *Status quaestionis*—until it was published in the *Tablet*, although Heenan presided over many meetings of the Commission in his capacity as one of its vice-presidents.[101] The members of the Commission did seem familiar with the document prepared favoring change. By contrast, it seems at least possible that *Status quaestionis* was never sent to the cardinals and bishops who were members of the Commission, or perhaps they did not have time to read to the bottom of the pile of documents sent to them.

[100] Hoyt, *Birth Control Debate*, 88–91.
[101] John Cardinal Heenan, "The Authority of the Church", *Tablet* 222 (May 18, 1968): 489.

What we have said should be enough to establish our point: The argument in sections II and III of the present article was not considered and answered by the theological *periti* who favored change in the papal Commission in 1966. They did consider the less adequate and less explicit formulation of this line of argument, but they did not squarely meet the argument even as it was then formulated. And there is some possibility that the bishops and cardinals who were members of the Commission did not even know about the argument as it was proposed in *Status quaestionis*.

The final point we wish to make in respect to the relationship between the position we are defending in the present article and the work of the papal Commission is that nothing in Paul VI's judgment upon the work of the Commission would have to be changed if the thesis we defend here were accepted. Of course, this point is obvious with respect to the Pope's refusal to accept the recommendation to approve the use of contraceptives and his reaffirmation of the traditional teaching in *Humanae vitae*. But there are other important aspects of the Commission's work which are less well known.

When the large group of experts who then constituted the Commission met in plenary session in March 1965, the theologians who considered change impossible were part of an important majority, among which there was consensus—although not on the substantive issue—at least upon the competence of the Magisterium to teach with authority on the matter of contraception. There was an important and substantial minority who maintained from the outset the a priori conviction that the received Catholic teaching was not infallible because it could not be so; they held that the Magisterium can at most give only prudential guidance on specific moral questions.[102] Paul VI's judgment on this theory is obvious from the style of teaching in *Humanae vitae* as well as from its substance. And this judgment is consistent with our conclusion that the received Catholic teaching has been proposed infallibly.

Again, in June 1964 the Commission was asked to consider the precise question of the "pill"; eventually all but one or two of the theological *periti* voted negatively on the question: "Whether in the moral consideration of methods the use of the 'pill' constitutes a special problem?"[103] *Humanae vitae* does not treat the contraceptive use of oral contraceptives as a special problem. The Pope finally became convinced that the possible opening he felt obliged to examine in 1964 was only apparent, not real. In this judgment also, Paul VI's conclusions are consistent with the thesis that the received Catholic teaching was proposed infallibly by the ordinary Magisterium, since oral contraceptives were always condemned, often specifically, as in *Si aliquis*.

---

[102] Henri de Riedmatten, O.P., "Report on the 4th Session of the Commission Set up by the Holy See to Study the Problems of Population, Family, and Birth-Rate (Rome; 25th to 28th March 1965)", mimeograph, English-language version, 39–40 and 45–46.

[103] Henri de Riedmatten, O.P., "Rapport Final", mimeograph with a covering letter dated June 27, 1966, pp. 8 and 18.

VI

If the received Catholic teaching on the morality of contraception has been proposed infallibly by the ordinary Magisterium, as we have argued, what is one to make of the reactions of Catholic bishops to *Humanae vitae*?

There were very many statements issued by individual bishops, particularly immediately after the publication of *Humanae vitae*. We know of no collection of this vast body of material. However, reports at the time in *L'Osservatore Romano* and in various news services indicated that almost all of these statements affirmed and many of them defended the teaching reaffirmed by the encyclical. Only a very few of these statements by individual Catholic bishops contained negative reactions, and even fewer went so far as to contradict what *Humanae vitae* reaffirmed.[104] State-

---

[104] The scantness of negative episcopal reaction can be seen by examining the *New York Times*, the *National Catholic Reporter*, and *NC News Service* from July 29 through Aug. 31, 1968; not more than a half-dozen negative reactions by individual bishops are reported. The media did not give equal attention to bishops who affirmed the teaching as their own and defended it against dissent. E.g., the booklet *Sex in Marriage: Love-giving, Life-giving*, originally published by Patrick Cardinal O'Boyle to instruct the faithful of his archdiocese, was reprinted with a personal commendation to their own faithful by the ordinaries of St. Louis, Philadelphia, Lafayette (Louisiana), St. Cloud, Sioux City, and Scranton. Many other ordinaries in the United States and Canada authorized the distribution of the booklet and ordered copies especially for the use of priests and teachers. The booklet also was published in New Zealand by the hierarchy of that country collectively. But the negative remarks

ments also were issued by or on behalf of various national hierarchies, and these statements have been collected.[105]

If one reviews the collective episcopal statements, it becomes clear that most of this body of teaching is consonant with the teaching of *Humanae vitae*. However, each of the documents has a unique character; all were composed as thoughtful responses both to the encyclical and to the pastoral problems raised by its reaffirmation of the received teaching.[106]

It is a mistake to speak of these episcopal statements as if they contributed a chorus of episcopal dissent to the dissent of some theologians, who criticized the encyclical and rejected its reaffirmation of the received teaching on contraception. None of the episcopal statements denied the competence of the Magisterium to propose specific moral norms, norms in themselves obligatory, on the morality of contraception. Moreover, none of the episcopal statements explicitly rejects the norms restated in *Humanae vitae*.[107]

The agreement between the bishops and Pope Paul

---

of one retired archbishop received more publicity than did this extensive effort to explain and defend *Humanae vitae*.

[105] E.g., by John Horgan, ed., *Humanae vitae and the Bishops: The Encyclical and the Statements of the National Hierarchies* (Shannon: Irish University, 1972). Even this collection is not complete. Cf. the list given by Martin Brugarola, S.J., "Presentación", in Zalba, *Las conferencias episcopales*, 5–7.

[106] Cf. E. Hamel, S.J., "Conferentiae episcopales et encyclica 'Humanae vitae'", in *De matrimonio coniectanea* (Rome: Gregorian University, 1970), 323–40.

[107] Ibid., 340.

was not merely tacit. Many of the hierarchies strongly and clearly affirm the competence of the Magisterium to propose norms and explicitly support the norms proposed in the encyclical. Almost all the rest make statements which—assuming as one should that they are sincere and are to be read in a straightforward sense—at least imply the competence of the Magisterium and imply that the bishops themselves agree with the received teaching. Thus Austin Flannery, O.P., observes:

> Two important points need to be emphasized about the divergences between the bishops' statements. The first is that no hierarchy fails to accept the encyclical. All of them accept it and all of them commend it to their people's acceptance. The second is that such divergences as there are, exist within the broader context of wholehearted acceptance of the main thrust of the encyclical's teaching on marriage.[108]

This observation seems to us correct. At the same time, we must also agree with Flannery that certain of the collective statements qualify the teaching in such a manner as implicitly to contradict it.[109]

These qualifications appear in the attempts of certain

[108] Austin Flannery, O.P., "Commentary or Qualification?" in Horgan, *Humanae vitae and the Bishops*, 355.

[109] Ibid., 366. See also Zalba, *Las conferencias episcopales*, chaps. on the statements of Belgium (59–72), Austria (90–100), Canada (112–21), Scandinavia (122–34), and France (141–59), as well as his "Conclusión" (182–93). Readers seeking a more adequate commentary on the collective statements than we are able to give here, yet consonant with the position we are defending, may study the whole of Zalba's detailed and balanced commentary.

hierarchies to mitigate pastorally the impact of the reaffirmation of the traditional teaching. Most of the collective statements do this in ways which neither contradict *Humanae vitae* nor distort common Catholic moral teaching upon the obligation of individuals to follow even an erroneous conscience and upon the possibility that subjective factors can and often do mitigate culpability for acts which are objectively grave. But a few of the statements try to go further, and if they do not implicitly deny that contraception always is gravely evil, they must be taken to imply the truly strange notion that what is objectively gravely evil might nevertheless be correctly judged to be permissible or even obligatory.

If there had *always* been teachings by Catholic bishops along these lines, the universality required for evidence of the infallible exercise of the ordinary Magisterium would never have been manifest. However, the implicit contradiction in 1968 by some bishops of a teaching already infallibly proposed through many centuries takes nothing away from the objective certitude of this teaching.

Moreover, just to the extent that some—and by far the minority—of the episcopal statements must be read as implying a view on the objective immorality of contraception different from the teaching reaffirmed in *Humanae vitae*, to the same extent these statements disagree with one another as well as with the majority of the episcopal statements which do not raise any problems. The statements which are not fully consonant with *Humanae vitae* and with the majority of the episcopal statements harmoniously responding to it also conflict with each other and tend to cancel each other out.

Some of the episcopal statements, while by no means stating or even implying that the bishops who joined in them dissented from the teaching of *Humanae vitae*, discuss the possibility and the limits of licit dissent from authoritative teachings of the Magisterium. In several cases such statements proceed directly from the nondefinitive character of *Humanae vitae* to the possibility of dissent. No hierarchy raises the question whether the received Catholic teaching has been proposed infallibly by the ordinary Magisterium, and so no hierarchy takes a position on this question. Hence, although what some of the hierarchies say about dissent seems to assume that the received teaching is not itself infallible, we see no warrant for supposing that bishops meant to take a position on this question to which they simply did not address themselves.

What should one make of the discussions of dissent in some of these episcopal statements? There are two possibilities. In some cases the discussion seems to be intended to point out that even if—an assumption but not a concession—the received teaching is only an authoritative, noninfallible one, still there are limits of dissent that must not be violated.[110] In other cases

---

[110] The collective pastoral of the U.S. hierarchy, *Human Life in Our Day*, Nov. 15, 1968, seems to us to require this interpretation. The discussion of dissent is headed "Norms of Licit *Theological* Dissent" (italics added); the bishops seem primarily concerned to criticize the dissent then occurring, even if the assumption of those dissenting that the teaching itself is noninfallible were granted.

hierarchies which argued directly from the nondefinitive character of *Humanae vitae* to the legitimacy of dissent obviously overlooked the possibility that the teaching is infallible even if the encyclical is not *ex cathedra*. In overlooking this possibility, these bishops shared in an erroneous assumption which prevailed at the time.

Since 1968, the Magisterium has continued to propose the received Catholic teaching on the morality of contraception and also has reaffirmed other moral teachings which have been called into question. Members of the pontifical Commission for the Study of Problems of Population, Family, and Birthrate who favored change in the received teaching concerning contraception believed that approval of contraception would not lead to the approval of other kinds of acts condemned until now by the Church as intrinsically evil. However, since 1968, many theologians who dissented from *Humanae vitae* have embraced positions in moral theory and in fundamental theology which seemed to them to justify their dissent and then have gone on to question or deny a wide range of received Catholic moral teachings. Uncertainty, confusion, and discouragement at the pastoral level seem to be increasing from year to year.

Our final conclusion is this. We think there is an extremely strong case for the position that the received Catholic teaching on the immorality of contraception has been infallibly proposed by the ordinary Magisterium. If the substantive issue were not so controversial, we think anyone who accepts what Vatican II has clearly articulated on the infallible exercise of the ordinary Magisterium would also admit that the history of the way in which the Church has proposed the teaching on contraception clearly shows that the criteria for infallibility have been met in this case.

What are the consequences if this thesis is admitted to be correct? Certain of the episcopal statements issued in response to *Humanae vitae* ought to be reconsidered. Much theological discussion of the past decade—not only concerning the received Catholic teaching on contraception but also concerning other teachings which perhaps have been proposed infallibly by the ordinary Magisterium—ought to be reevaluated. Perhaps most important, pastoral practice ought to be reviewed and reformed to the extent necessary in order to bring it into better harmony with the Church's moral teaching.

But the concern of bishops to mitigate as much as possible the impact at the pastoral level of received moral teaching perhaps points to the need and the possibility of authentic development with respect to the subjective factors which limit culpability. Recent theological discussion, in its abundance and diversity, perhaps contains the seminal ideas required for such development. Moreover, if pastoral practice were reviewed and reformed to bring practice into conformity with irreformable teaching, still it would be impossible to go too far in understanding and in genuinely Christ-like compassion toward the faithful who have suffered so much and in so many ways in the confusion since 1963.